The M Club Manual

The M Club Manual

Missions, Memos, Mandates, Mottos, and More

Kathryn Sultzbaugh

**Andrews McMeel
Publishing**

Kansas City

The M Club Manual © 2004 by Kathryn Sultzbaugh.
All rights reserved. Printed in the United States
of America. No part of this book may be used or
reproduced in any manner whatsoever without written
permission except in the case of reprints in the context
of reviews. For information, write Andrews McMeel
Publishing, an Andrews McMeel Universal company,
4520 Main Street, Kansas City, Missouri 64111.

04 05 06 07 08 MLT 10 9 8 7 6 5 4 3 2 1

Library of Congress Cataloging-in-Publication Data

Sultzbaugh, Kathryn.
  The M club manual : missions, memos, mandates,
mottos & more / Kathryn Sultzbaugh.
    p. cm.
  ISBN 0-7407-4719-3
    1. Women—United States. I. Title.

HQ1410.S85 2004
305.4'0973—dc22   2004044895

ATTENTION: SCHOOLS AND BUSINESSES

Andrews McMeel books are available at quantity discounts
with bulk purchase for educational, business, or sales
promotional use. For information, please write to: Special
Sales Department, Andrews McMeel Publishing, 4520 Main
Street, Kansas City, Missouri 64111.

For Anne

CONTENTS

iNTRODUCTiON

Public Announcement

From: The M Club

Dateline America—This is a public announcement to inform Americans of a new women's club. Of course, the best way to get news out is to publish a book, so nobody will have an excuse for not hearing about The M Club. We are sick and tired of excuses.

We are not really a new club. We have been around for a long time. Our membership includes millions of women of various ages, from early thirties to late eighties and up. The U.S. Census says there are around forty million women in our group, so that is the number of women in The M Club. We are not like any other club. We do not keep a list of members. We are sick and tired of lists. There is no registration to be in The M Club because we are also sick and tired of keeping track. We have kept track of our children, our husbands, our medical records, our tax returns, and shoes for other people. We don't keep track anymore.

M Club members are women who have taken care of everything for a long time. There are no dues to be in The M Club because our members have already paid their dues. We have taken care of the health and happiness of our families, our relatives, our friends, and sometimes even strangers. We were at the bottom of that list of those we took care of for many, many years. Now we have time to take care of ourselves, as well as a few things that have been bothering us for a while.

Our members have the experience and tenacity to find solutions for any type of problem because no matter *what* else we were all doing, we took care of a *lot* of business! This is where we got all of our experience.

While taking care of some of these things around here, M Club members do other things, like: work at paying positions, work at nonpaying positions, manage households including husbands and children, manage households for ourselves and a pet, get married or get divorced, enjoy the company of a big group of friends or enjoy one friend who is so special we feel lucky just to have one, do a lot of traveling or stay close to home, gain some weight or lose some weight, laugh a lot or cry sometimes.

Women like us have so many things in common we ought to have *a club!* So now we do: The M Club.

We know there are already a lot of clubs. There are some very old clubs around too, like those that call themselves a "league" and are fussy about the way they dress and are awfully concerned about the amount of money they have. Those kinds of clubs feel they have the right to choose who gets into their club and who they don't want in their club.

The M Club isn't fussy or choosy. We don't care about money or clothes. M Club members just don't think these things are as important as other things. We don't exclude anyone either. We feel we are all in this together so we may as well be in the same club. Besides, even though we have a lot of differences, M Club members feel the same about a *lot* of things, including, but not limited to:

- We are sick and tired (mostly tired) of things in general going to hell in a handbasket.

- We are intelligent, savvy women who know right from wrong.

- We are polite.

- We are consistently nonviolent.

- We stick up for each other because we understand, we are compassionate, and we may have been in the same situation ourselves.

- We help other M Club members because we want to and we are able to.

- Sometimes we have to "come over there" to help another member. Often, we "go over there" together, in a big group, so we can make an impression.

- M Club members often take care of things individually, but it is always nice to know there are forty million other women in the Club who may be called on for help or support anytime.

In case anyone is wondering why we are called The M Club, we say: *Why not?* The letter "M" is almost in the middle of the alphabet. M Club members are somewhere in the middle of our lives, so we *know* what is going on, have already been through a lot, and have firm ideas about how to handle things because of our experience.

We are magical, we manage, and we are a majority. We make sense, make time, make ends meet, make headway, and make good on promises. We maneuver, we mandate, we march, and we market. We are marvels of martyrdom. We are masters en masse as well as matriarchs. We are matter-of-fact, mature, and at our maximum power, if you care to measure.

We can be mellow or melodramatic, meek, modest, or menacing, and sometimes these traits seem to meld together. We are mild and mighty, methodical and merry. We make mistakes, get mixed up, are misunderstood, and are moderately modern. We are a mix of moral monarchs who are sick and tired of monkey business, and we intend to modify some of the things we see wrong around here, when the mood strikes. Speaking of moods, sometimes our moods swing out of control, a fact that will be addressed later. We are a movement that is underway in a multitude of places with a myriad of mutual like-mindedness. It's no mystery. We are all in this together.

Maybe you would like to *join the Club*. Meanwhile, The M Club will be taking care of a *lot* of business because *it is our business*. Sick and tired? Join the Club!

All best,

M Club President

CHAPTER 1

M Club President
Official Bio and Résumé

NAME: Choose any female name you want. I don't care what you call me.

AGE: Between thirty-two and eighty-eight, and up.

CURRENT OCCUPATION: Same as it was when I focused on my family and friends and took care of all their needs, health, and happiness for the past twenty-five years. I have worked at a variety of paying positions too. I have made a lot of money or not much money. I have a little education or I have degrees all over the wall, framed. I am also in charge of shoes, apparently, because people I live with always ask me where their shoes are located. Currently, I am performing many similar tasks for the forty million women in The M Club. Well, everything except the shoe job. We know where our shoes are.

EXPERIENCE: *A lot.* I am the woman in front of you at the checkout line who is flushed, sighing heavily, and close to tears because her husband used the last check in the checkbook and the $140 worth of groceries is already bagged up and back in the cart. This was not a very big problem, compared with being pulled into a separate room (all alone and under tremendous suspicion) when I explained to the emergency room doctor that my kid really *was* so uncoordinated that he broke his collarbone while racing his brother in the grassy yard.

I am the woman who stopped to wait with the young woman with the flat tire in a scary section of downtown. I waited with her while she was on hold with the roadside assistance company for fifteen minutes. I waited with her for another half-hour after the company said someone was coming to help. She kept saying I didn't have to wait with her, that she was not afraid. But I know she was because her little hand holding the cell phone was shaking. I finally changed the damn tire myself. I taught her how to change a tire. Then I got a refund from the roadside assistance company for the $236.87 she had paid in premiums. I made them buy me a new coat because I got axle grease on mine when I changed her tire. They couldn't believe how expensive microfiber is!

I am the woman in the magazine aisle at the drugstore who told the ten-year-old boy to *move.* His mother was dressed in her office clothes and had her hands full of stuff for his dinner. I heard her ask him, "Come on, honey, Daddy will be home in ten minutes and I still have to fix dinner and wash your Little League uniform." Of course, I kept quiet. But when he continued to ignore her and picked up another motorcycle magazine, I was forced to speak up. Using a clenched jaw and gritting my teeth, I said in an even tone, "Do not make your mother ask you again." Then I gave him *The M Club Glare.* I am experienced in getting my messages across with an economy of words.

I am the woman Michelle called when that construction company parked in her handicap space at the school for the second time. She had called the construction office after the first time and told the secretary she volunteered at the school a *lot* and she had only one leg. Michelle told the girl those construction guys were young and they could certainly park someplace else. When they blocked her space again, Michelle called me. I called the company president. I demanded an apology for Michelle. I told him he should also send flowers to her at the school. I told him he had better make sure her handicap space was clear when she went to pick up her flowers and that the flowers had better be there by 3:00 p.m. EST on Monday. The space has been kept clear, but no flowers were sent by the deadline. I am *going over there* to the construction company office later today.

I am the woman who caused a scene at the small-town festival in September. A green truck was blocking the alley when I went to pick up the kids, who had been selling soda from a cooler on a wagon for a school fund-raiser.

When a twenty-year-old boy walked up to put something in the green truck, I asked him politely to pull on through the alley. I explained that I couldn't back up because the kids and wagons with coolers were behind me. He said he couldn't pull through. He wouldn't even try. I tried to explain again. Then he made a big mistake.

"Oh, so you want to have a little attitude with me, honey?"

I turned the car off and took the keys, because I have never left children in a car while it is running. The young man looked surprised when I said, "Yes," and went over there. I could tell he was surprised because his mouth was open and his eyes got big when he saw me *comin' over there.* He looked a lot like that ten-year-old at the drugstore. After a little chat, he proved he indeed *could* pull through and unblock the alley very easily.

I am the woman who calls her friends and asks, "Am I insane and will you still love me if I am?" Then I listen to a story about what happened to them and it sounds a lot like my stories.

I am the woman who doesn't care much about my weight or looks anymore. I have been a lot bigger and I have been a lot smaller than I am now. So what? I look different than I did a year ago and I will look different next year. I don't care much what my friends look like either. I see who they are through their eyes and right down into their hearts. I look at other people like that too; it is *in* their eyes, not *around* their eyes.

I laugh a lot and I cry sometimes. I am motivated and

I am lazy. I care immensely and sometimes I just don't care. I will find out anything for you, but I will also show you how to find out yourself.

I am patient.
I am impatient.
I am healthy and vibrant.
Sometimes I am sick and tired.
I am you.

CHAPTER 2

Are You *in* The M Club?

by The M Club President

Listen up, America. We have plenty of problems right now, but there is another threat you need to be aware of. If you haven't heard, there are more middle-aged women in this country than ever before.

Because of so many women M-powered by Experience, we have formed The M Club.

We know there are already a lot of clubs. First, there is *The Idiot Girl's Action Adventure Club* (Villard), and now St. Martin's Press is publishing *The Dirty Girl's Social Club*. Members of The M Club are not dirty girls or idiots. We are a separate club.

I have never been a club joiner myself, after a couple of bad experiences. Years ago, I had tried to join the volunteer club at the elementary school, thinking my children would take pride in their working mother who was involved in their education.

I had signed up to read valentines to my son's kindergarten class, attend the party, and help serve red drinks and pink heart-shaped cookies. Unfortunately, the calendar where I kept vital information and reminders for a family of five had been buried under a pile of papers, junk mail, and bills on the kitchen counter since just after Christmas, so I had forgotten that I had a dental appointment scheduled for the same day as the party. Also unfortunately, I was still in that little publicized and brief stage of my life when I was under the impression I could "do it all." After the dental appointment and the school volunteer job, I had also planned to do my taxes.

So I showed up at school with a lip full of Novocain and drooled and lisped my way through the best I could. The teachers and other volunteer mothers probably thought I was drunk. I tried to explain, but how convincing can a person be when their eyes are watering uncontrollably and a smile meant to reassure them is lopsided? There still are rumors flying around that school about me. I deserve it though. Other mothers are, I'm sure, better at scheduling things. They post their calendars where they can find them. They can even find a pencil.

My point is, I don't like clubs but I'm convinced of the need for one now. So I started a club for all of these millions of women who have taken care of a *lot* of things, basically all of us. We should have a logo of some kind, because companies use logos and are very successful at getting their names out there for recognition. Without a logo, senior club members could recognize each other only by the bumpy, wrinkly skin on our elbows. Junior members could be recognized only by our lack of a waistline. But because many irritatingly youthful-looking women insist on staying in shape, you can't always tell by a woman's appearance whether or not she is in The M Club.

Our logo is the letter "M" carried on a card or embroidered somewhere on our clothing. We wear the letter "M" anywhere we feel like it, because some of us are cranky. The M Club insignia is sometimes visible, but it doesn't have to be.

Our club motto is "We are coming into our own." This is a statement Americans must not take lightly. We have put up with a lot over the years, and now we are sick and tired (mostly tired) of everything going to hell in a handbasket. We are united in our determination to see some changes around here.

We have accumulated the experience, tenacity, and skills to take care of everything and everyone, and now we are branching out. M Club members are imaginative. Of course, some of us are basically paranoid because we have lived with teenagers.

We are a group of around forty million women of various ages and backgrounds. We don't keep track of the exact number of members because we are sick and tired of *keeping track*. We have kept track of our children, our husbands, our medical records, our tax returns, and shoes for other people.

M Club members' names aren't on any kind of list, either. We are sick and tired of lists too.

Our suggestion is for *all* Americans to educate them-selves about the many aspects of women like us. Educa-tion is always a good defense, in our opinion.

Our M Club code of ethics is pretty strict. We don't use physical violence at any time. However, we are not immune to reminding others, especially young mothers, that God Almighty fashioned the earlobe of a child not for piercing but as a means of getting a person's attention.

We are not loud. By our very nature, we are too tired to shout. We have also fine-tuned the art of using as few words as possible to get our message across. Our messages are usually delivered in an even tone, with an economy of words, and whether or not we use a clenched jaw and/or grit our teeth is entirely dependent on your infraction.

We are polite. M Club members have dealt with far greater challenges before, when we had patience and love in our hearts for all mankind.

We are in a more powerful position now because we have more money. We are no longer choosing between a pair of size-four sneakers and a rump roast for Sunday dinner. Our kids are buying their own shoes now, and, if we're lucky, a pair for us once in a while. (This is an un-confirmed report from the Bloomington, Indiana, chapter of The M Club.) We are careful with our money because of all our years of experience of paying the bills with too little money. We are also finally buying items for our-selves after years of sacrificing money for everyone else's wants and needs. Frankly, if clerks at any type of store want to give us a hassle over a return of merchandise, an item left at the register on a previous shopping trip that was paid for and didn't make it home, or our inability to provide a receipt, you are just asking for trouble. M Club members sometimes shop in pairs, and you really don't want to argue with two or more members of The M Club. Suffice it to say, you will lose.

Along with strict ethics, M Club members are working on a project that may change family life as we know it. We have created and will be distributing a series of audio-tapes and CDs featuring the worn-out lectures we have given through the years. Subscribers will choose from:

The "Why You Can't Take My Car" lecture, accompanied by Beach Boys background music

The "Of Course It Is Your Decision, But If I Were You . . ." lecture (includes three "I Told You So" gift cards)

A short audio to play when anyone in the family asks "Where is my —— ?"

The long version of "I'll Tell You Why I Seem Flushed and Cranky" speech

An abridged "After All I Have Done for You" lecture, available in both "husband" or "child" format

The M Club is growing by leaps and bounds and will have more titles available soon. With all the time we save using the recorded lectures alone, M Club members will be taking it easy because we deserve it. We will also be unleashed from many of the restraints on our time, and we may very well be traveling to *your* state in the very near future. We are giving you fair warning, America. The M Club may be *comin' over there* to a city or town near you very soon (or as soon as we feel like it).

Joining the Club is easy. There is no registration. There are no dues. We have all paid our dues. Members' names don't need to be kept track of on any type of list. We are sick and tired of lists. We are also sick and tired of keeping track. We have kept track of our children, our husbands, our medical records, and shoes for other people. In fact, we don't even have any charters or bylaws to keep track of.

We all know the bylaws of The M Club. We are intelligent, honest, decent women. We know right from wrong. And we see a lot of things that are wrong, and we are doing something about them.

And we aren't mad as hell all the time. We write a lot of letters or "go over there" to thank people for doing it right, for going above and beyond the call of duty, and for helping each other out. Sara Martin, M Club vice president, came up with a new project of making "above and beyond the call of duty" the norm, when everyone will give their best effort all the time. She is an optimistic woman, but we think this project might take a while.

Mostly we are enjoying this time of our lives. We did the best job we could for a lot of years. Now we are taking on new challenges. We are using the experience we have garnered from all the years of lessons learned and Herculean effort to make everything work out okay. We have done a good job. Of course, there is much more to do.

Everyone is invited to join. Remember, there are no dues because we have all paid our dues. There is no registration because we are sick and tired of lists. If a person wants to be in The M Club, she is *in*. And if there is anything you need any help with, just e-mail the Club. We will help. We sincerely hope you will join the Club. Bless your hearts.

M CLUB TITLES AND POSITIONS

Like other "clubs," we have many different positions and titles for our members. Unlike other clubs, a position in The M Club carries absolutely no responsibility. We are sick and tired of responsibility.

When you join The M Club, it is up to you to appoint yourself a title. Please choose whatever position you want. Choosing a position or title does not obligate you. Change your title as often as you change your hair color if you want. Keep the same title as long as you keep a favorite outfit that you hope to fit into again. We don't care. Just be sure to *act* like an M Club member, which of course is what you are already doing. And be sure to let your fellow M Club members know if you need help on anything. We will be glad to help. This is also what we have all already been doing, and that's why we are so good at it.

A woman might be in The M Club if she is in favor of saving time. We are experienced at taking care of many things simultaneously and have worked out certain shortcuts for ourselves. Some of us have been forced to work out these time-saving ideas because there have never been and will never be enough hours in the day for us to accomplish all the tasks we are in charge of.

Take this handy M Club quiz to find out if you are in favor of saving time:

1. Have you ever cleaned the bathtub and/or shower while you are *in* the bathtub/shower?

    a. Sometimes.

    b. Yes, but I don't brag about it.

    c. I am sick and tired of cleaning the tub.

2. Do you wait until you have at least three errands to do so you can save time and effort instead of making special trips and wearing yourself out?

    a. Yes, but I still wear myself out.

    b. I am sick and tired of errands.

    c. Yes, and that is the reason my friends and I are petitioning the public library and video rental place to do away with their unfair "late fee" policy.

3. What do you do with all the time you save?

    a. Sit on a chaise lounge in the green, green grass and sip a Tequila Sunrise with a little umbrella in it.

    b. Take a nap so I'm able to keep going until midnight, when I can be found folding laundry in front of the television.

    c. I have not saved any time yet, but I'm still hoping to.

One example of an M Club title is Treasurer. Do you have a friend whose humor and friendship you absolutely treasure? As treasurer, she does not have to keep track of money or anything like that. Most of us have some money. We never have enough money, but, like that time thing, M Club members have enough for the important things.

There are M Club "Ambassador" titles available too. Do you have a friend who seems to be an ambassador of goodwill wherever she goes?

Our first M Club ambassador is Debi Patterson. "I am thrilled and pleased with this appointment," Debi said, "but I believe the correct term for a woman ambassador is 'Ambassadress.' However, I will stick with 'Ambassador' because 'Ambassadress' sounds like what happened when I tried to wiggle into my favorite dress, which is two sizes too small now."

We have M Club VIP positions available. We have as many vice presidents, CEO positions, and executive positions as there are women interested in being in The M Club. Choose your own title, by all means. Choose a title today by 5:00 p.m. EST.

"*Join the Club!*"

Let us know of a fellow M Club member's outstanding performance or opinion on any issue. Send your rants, press releases, inventions, consumer news, advice, candidate for M Club celebrity interview, questions, and answers to M Club headquarters at TheMClub@aol.com. And don't forget: we are all in this together. Thanks.

"*Choose your own title.*
Do we have to do everything?"

ARE YOU iN THE M CLUB?

Women in The M Club understand and help each other. Our members have taken care of our children, husbands, friends, relatives, and many other people for many, many years. We give gifts from the heart. It is a rare occurrence to hear an M Club member ask another member, "What do you want for your birthday?" We don't need to ask. We remember a comment from a friend made months ago concerning something that would make her happy or brighten her life. M Club members can't remember where the car keys are or what time that dental appointment we just scheduled is, but we remember what will make a friend happy.

You might be in The M Club if you have ever done something like this for a friend:

It Was No Trouble at All . . .
Because She's My Friend
by Christina Wertz

My friend of twenty-five years, Debi, was poor when I was poor and also raised three sons while I was raising my three sons. Her husband dropped dead of a heart attack at age forty-two, almost five years ago. When she met and married a wonderful man, I helped her move out of her old, run-down farmhouse. She lives in a big new house now.

About eight weeks ago, she came over, sat down, and cried. She said the property she used to live on had been annexed to the MetroPark and that her old house had been sold at auction for $10 and was going to be moved.

"Why is this upsetting you so much, honey?" I asked. "You have a nice house now, and we packed up all the good memories when we moved you out of there."

"But *why* didn't I take that piece of wood from the kitchen doorjamb, the one I marked the heights of all the boys on as they grew?" she wailed. "Their measurements on that wood go back to a time when I was a young mother, before Tom died, when we were all together as a family," she said. "I wish I'd gotten that before I moved. Now it is lost forever."

I poured the coffee and Debi went to the bathroom to blow her nose. She changed the subject when she came back in for her coffee.

It took me seven weeks, eighteen phone calls, four appointments, and a little resourcefulness (I finally had to go over there) to get that piece of wood for my friend. Jeff and I presented it to her on her forty-eighth birthday, November 26. It was not wrapped. It was banged up and pitted, with wall-trim paint in an assortment of colors near the edges. The first entry at the lowest point said "Ben 4-8-76" with a pencil line underneath. The mark was so close to the floor that that kid must have wobbled on toddler legs as Debi helped him stand there for the measurement. There were ink, pencil, and marker marks for Brad and Gordy. When she couldn't find a pencil, Debi carved a line into the wood and etched the date and name.

The forty-nine marks on that piece of wood are a testament to Debi's mothering through difficult times over many years. The last entry, at the very top, is Ben's again. He was more than six feet tall, and it was more than ten years ago. Ben plays professional baseball now.

The boys, home for Thanksgiving, spent hours examining the beat-up old doorjamb and talking about their childhoods: skating on the pond near the old farmhouse, playing hockey and baseball with their dad, and camping out in the woods. They spoke of the way they could count on Debi to be in that kitchen, always ready with something to eat for her boys. They talked about their dad too; his handwriting had marked a few of the entries of their growth on that old kitchen trim.

I might have bought Debi a sweater for her forty-eighth birthday, but I chose a better gift for her . . . because she's my friend. It wasn't any trouble at all.

Have you done something special for a friend? Send us your story! E-mail it to TheMClub@aol.com. And remember, we're all in this together. Thanks.

CHAPTER 3

Beauty

M Club members have lived long enough to understand that it is inner beauty that counts. In fact, we are currently tracking down the person who first said "Age before beauty" while holding a door open for a woman. We intend to have a little chat with that person. Of course, M Club members know it does not matter how old a person is or what a person looks like, for beauty is not an attribute that can be seen from the outside.

What if there were as many magazines, books, and commercial products concentrating on "inner beauty" as there are devoted to beauty as it is currently defined? What if everyone woke up tomorrow and realized that the millions of dollars spent on creams, lotions, regimens, and advice was all a great big waste of time and money?

"We've been fat and
we've been thin.
So what?"

"Skin is skin. So what?"

"Beauty is *not* in the eye
of the beholder.
Behold yourself.
Then act accordingly."

The M Club takes care of some of our business by writing letters to individuals. We are resourceful women who know how to find out who is in charge. We always start at the top, because the person in charge is the one most likely to be able to make the decision. Of course, in case we need to do further explaining (in the form of a little chat), we are always prepared to *go over there.*

"We are comin' over there.
We have cars."

M Club Memo

To: Oil of Olay
Att: Alan Lafley, President and CEO
Re: Your lotions and expensive face creams

Alan:

Please take out the ingredient in your face lotion that makes our eyes sting. Take it out by 5:00 p.m. EST today.

Don't give us that excuse about having a warning notice on the pink bottle to keep the stuff away from our eyes. Alan, I defy you to put some Oil of Olay on your own face and *never* get *any* in or near your eyes.

Speaking of "defy," please take the phrase "age defying" off of the damn label. You are not selling any more Oil of Olay by claiming this kind of thing. We buy it because we like pink. That's all.

Alan, The M Club is a group of *forty million women* who are sick and tired of our eyes stinging. We are defying *age* all by ourselves and we don't need your help, thank you.

So just *walk* down there to the factory, or wherever you mix up the enormous batches of the stuff, and make them take out that stinging ingredient. Then, *walk* over there to the printer and get that "age-defying" phrase off the label. Do it today, Alan. Do it by 5:00 p.m. EST.

If you do not agree to our simple request, you will have to think of something else to do with the millions of gallons of the pink moisturizer, because *we* will not be buying it anymore. Who knows, maybe you could sell it as a floor polish. We might even defy you to prove the claims you make about defying age. We will do this defying in the *New York Times*.

We don't really care what you do with the millions of gallons we won't be buying. But if you don't want to lose M Club women as customers, you should get moving, Alan.

Thanks,
The M Club

P.S.: Do not change the color when you make the other requested changes. We like pink.

In case you didn't know, a "press release" containing important information or news is submitted to newspapers and magazines in an effort to inform a *lot* of people at the same time. Newspapers publish press releases and sometimes follow up with a feature story for their papers. Because M Club members are in favor of efficiency, we issue a *lot* of press releases. That way, we can get our messages out through newspapers. Look for future M Club press releases in your local paper in The M Club's syndicated column distributed by Universal Press Syndicate.

Press Release
For Immediate Release
April 22, 2004

In case you didn't know, or used to know but somehow forgot, members of The M Club have ignored "fighting the signs of aging" for many years. As a direct result, we want any and all print ads, television commercials for any type of age-defying product, books, internet articles, etc. (you get the idea), to cease and desist using the phrase "fights the signs of aging" in any and all ad campaigns. The M Club wants this ceasing and desisting to begin today by 6:00 p.m. EST.

We don't care if two twenty-year-old girls talk about it, but they should not talk about it around an M Club member. This may be difficult, because there are forty million women in The M Club and you never can tell who is in the Club just by looking at her.

We do not owe an explanation of this new mandate, but we thought it would be helpful to give a few clues to highlight our position:

1. M Club members have a *lot* of other things to fight besides "the signs of aging." We read the newspapers and are informed of many problems around here that could be solved if someone, anyone, stepped in and solved the problem. For instance, M Club members believe some hungry children could be fed with all the oatmeal that is being suggested for facial treatments to "fight the signs of aging." We think oatmeal, almond oil, and yogurt ought to be used as a breakfast for a hungry person instead of mixed up and spread all over the face. Likewise with cucumber slices and tea bags, which we are told to put on our eyes. A cucumber sandwich (with the crusts cut off) and a cup of tea would be the highlight of the day for most women living in a nursing home. The M Club believes that cucumber slices and tea bags ought to be used to fight *loneliness* instead of signs of aging.

2. Despite continuing advertising, the cosmetics companies are losing the battle trying to sell M Club members lotions or creams to help us "fight the signs of aging." We don't care about the signs of aging. We care that too much money is being spent to produce, market, and advertise cute little jars of stuff that stings our eyes for exorbitant prices while good teachers are being paid so little money to shape the future of America.

3. M Club members have been too busy to notice any "signs of aging" in the physical sense. We have

been fighting the status quo on things that have gotten out of hand around here that no one was doing anything about for years and years.

4. The fighting we have been doing may or may not have caused those "signs of aging" that manufacturers seem to think we are all so worried about. As far as we know, the number of days a person lives is the direct cause of "signs of aging," and we need some way of showing other people that we have lived long enough to know what we are talking about. We have been taking care of our husbands, our children, our tax and medical records, and shoes for other people for a long time. M Club members have a *lot* of experience and tenacity, know right from wrong, and are willing to help. We know how to solve problems quickly and efficiently. We use an economy of words. And we use those signs of aging to back up our ideas. We don't fight our signs of aging!

5. Fighting signs of aging with any product, book, article, or unwanted telemarketing phone call is not on The M Club agenda, so all you people who think we are interested in your spiel need to know that *you are fighting a losing battle.* Stop it. Stop it today by 6:00 p.m. EST or *The M Club is comin' over there.*

6. Please be prepared with a few ideas on worthy battles that there is a chance of winning when The M Club comes over there. If you don't think of some yourselves, we will bring assignments for you all and tell you which fights The M Club needs help on,

including but not limited to poverty, education, courts that keep finding murderers not guilty, hunger, and so on.

See you soon!
The M Club

P.S.: In case you didn't know, or used to know but somehow forgot, skin is skin. Skin with *or* without "signs of aging" turns to dust in the end.

M Club Celebrity Interview

Today's celebrity is forty-five-year-old
Gerty Holzenberger from Savannah, Georgia.

M CLUB PRESIDENT: Thank you for joining us today, Gerty, to discuss your recent traumatic experience at a department store cosmetics counter.

GERTY: You're welcome. If I can spare just one other woman the pain and humiliation I went through, I feel my story will be worthwhile.

M CLUB PRESIDENT: Tell us what happened, in your own words.

GERTY: I went to a fancy department store cosmetics counter for the first time in my life. Sure, I had walked past those counters many times, but I was always too intimidated by the perfect-looking women behind the array of expensive perfumes, makeups named Merle, and gadgets I didn't have a clue what to do with. I also thought I was too young to worry about the ravages of age and what they had been secretly doing to my face. Besides, I didn't have the kind of money it took to buy a $26 lipstick when I knew very well I could buy two pairs of sneakers for the boys with that money.

But now I had a reason to go to one of these slick cosmetic counters. I had seen an ad for a Mother's Day special for perfume on sale for $50. The ad had come to the house with one of those "pull here to experience the alluring scent" paper perfume samples. I pulled it open and sniffed. I liked it very much. But even a woman who doesn't visit cosmetics counters knows that every perfume reacts with a woman's own pheromones to create an individual and exclusive scent, uniquely her own. To get the true scent, it would have to react with my own body chemistry. So I rubbed the paper briskly on my neck and throat so I could really experience the fragrance.

The paper-cut slash under my chin was just healing when I made my way to the department store cosmetics counter. I have money now because those boys are buying their own shoes. Also, I am not intimidated by flawless-looking women anymore. I figure that if they've spent so much time battling the ravages of aging for the last decade, they have missed out on a lot of things I got to do when I was totally ignoring the sands of time marching across my face.

Anyway, what I really had come for, in addition to the perfume, was the lovely free gift with my purchase. It was a five-piece porcelain picture frame set with pretty flowers embellishing the frames. One of the five pieces was actually a little clock, not a picture frame, but I could always use another clock. The free gift set was a $49 value! So you could say that I went to buy the porcelain frames and clock and I was getting the perfume for free. What a deal!

It's not that I don't appreciate all the Mother's Day gifts I have received from my sons over the years. I do. In fact, I use many of the handmade cards as bookmarks and am still amused at the perceptions these kids had of their mother when they were five- and six-year-olds. I am depicted with purple hair in some of the drawings. In others, I have no neck. Other previous gifts include the crepe-paper roses on wire stems with the toilet-paper-roll vase that I still keep on my bedside table. These will always be among my favorites.

This year I was buying my own Mother's Day gift and telling the boys what they got for me.

I took a seat at the cosmetics counter and a woman appeared instantly. She was wearing a white coat, like a nurse or some other kind of professional. She was older than me and wore full face makeup.

"What can I do for you today?" she asked sweetly, positioning two 100-watt lightbulbs to point in my eyes.

"I am buying myself a Mother's Day present and I want this perfume," I told her, pulling out the bloodstained paper sample that I had gotten in the mail. "Here it is, the one with the porcelain picture frames as my free gift."

"Jane!" yelled the white-coated woman, across the aisle. "Bring me a bottle of that Allure that's on special."

Then, turning back to me, she said, "While we wait for Jane, do you mind if I ask you a question?"

"Not at all," I said. "But first, can you turn out those lights you've got shining on me? They are about to bring on a hot flash."

She flipped on two more 150-watt bulbs.

"Ma'am, have you taken a really good look at your skin lately?" she asked, blinking her eyes, heavy with mascara. "The question I want to ask you is this: You spent a lot of time in the sun over the last ten years, am I right?"

I may have jumped a little when she thrust the oval mirror in front of me.

"Well, yes, I did," I replied. "We had a pool to keep the boys busy during the summer."

The cosmetics woman shook her head and started making an annoying tisking sound.

"I couldn't very well let them drown, could I? *Of course* I was out in the sun—watching the kids!" I said, defensively.

She continued to shake her head and tisk. Then she pulled a pointer out of her lab coat pocket and almost poked me in the eye with it.

"Just look at these lines around your eyes!" she said. "If you don't do something *right now, today,* you will be very sorry."

I was already sorry. I was sorry I had come to this cosmetics counter. I was even sorrier that the mirror she had up against my face magnified about 100 times normal and that I was seeing not only all the lines around my eyes but also, thanks to the lighting, I was also seeing about six coarse, dark chin hairs. One was so long I knew it had to have been there for a while.

"Look, I'm only interested in buying the perfume," I said, my face getting red. "And don't forget the free gift, a $49 value."

She must have pressed a secret, hidden button under the counter or something, because two other white-coated women suddenly appeared. With all of them dressed in white coats like that, I had the feeling they were the "emergency crew" called in to help with a particularly difficult case.

"You know, with a little color and a basic skin-care regime, you may be able to recapture your youth," said Sally. Her name tag said she was a five-year employee. "Look at this new antigravity eye cream we have for you," she said. "It's fragrance free, allergy tested, and guaranteed!"

The other emergency-team member was dipping some out on a cotton swab and going for my eye with it.

"If one of you ladies comes at my eyes with anything sharp again, I am going to scream," I shouted, standing up. "I was poked in the eye by my son when he was three, trying to take a stick away from him before he hit his brother!" I said. "I don't *want* to recapture my youth. I want a decent Mother's Day present, which I am buying for myself, and *I want my free gift, a $49 value!*"

Just then, Jane crossed the aisle with the perfume. I took the box of picture frames from the display. The white-coated women melted away to other counters. They did not tell me to "come back soon."

I have decided not to approach a cosmetics counter again. First of all, the little porcelain clock is so loud I can't keep it on my bedside table. Second, those lights did bring on a hot flash—I think the Food and Drug Administration ought to be notified about them. And finally, I haven't been able to wear eye makeup since I started bursting into tears over the slightest insults. So I won't be purchasing any cosmetics anyway.

I am also very dissatisfied with the perfume. It doesn't smell at all like the paper sample did. I must have been rubbing the glue from the sample all over my neck. And that glue may have been made with some special ingredient, because now I have coarse, black hairs starting to grow on my neck. I'll just bet the FDA would like to know about that too!

M CLUB PRESIDENT: Thank you for sharing your story today, Gerty.

GERTY: Thank you for the opportunity to say, "Skin is skin—so what!"

M CLUB VOTING RESULTS

The results are in on our recent survey on beauty. The M Club polled our forty million members and asked: "What do you do about signs of aging?"

A whopping 85 percent said, "I enjoy them. When I am laughing with a girlfriend, the sparkle in her eyes is highlighted by the delicious lines around her eyes and I remember we have laughed together for years and years."

Another 8 percent of those polled said, "I must have been busy because I haven't noticed. Besides, I have an age spot that looks almost exactly like the state of Ohio and I think it's pretty special."

Five percent of those polled said they are doing everything humanly possible to erase the signs of aging. "Having my face sandpapered until it looks like prosciutto, and being repeatedly stuck in the forehead with a needle for Botox injections, is a small price to pay for getting carded when I bought some wine!"

The remaining percentage of M Club members said they would vote after they slept on it, and apparently took a nice long nap.

Signs of Aging Poll

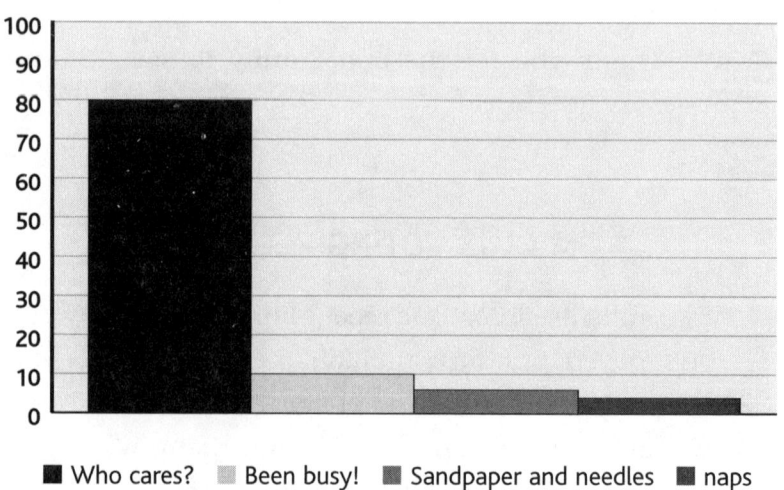

■ Who cares? ▨ Been busy! ▥ Sandpaper and needles ■ naps

In another survey, M Club members were asked, "How did you get these signs of aging?"

Results are as follows:

Figure 1: Where Did We Get Signs of Aging?

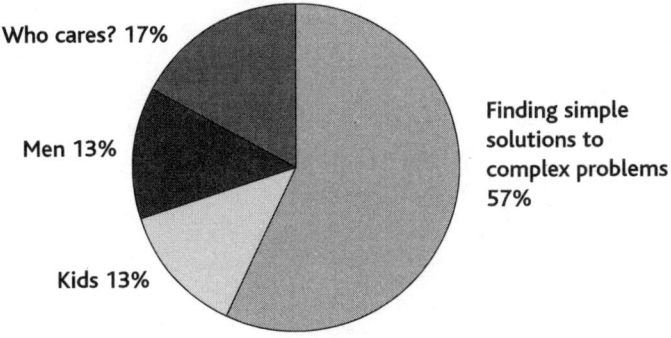

CHAPTER 4

Finding Simple Solutions
to Complex Problems

M Club members are sick and tired of everything being so complicated. We are complicated women with a *lot* of ideas on how to solve problems simply and effectively. We have had to do this for many years, and we have gotten good at it. We are also able to get to the heart of the matter and clearly see what needs to be done. We have hearts.

The following is a collection of M Club letters, rants, and recipes on boiling down stuff for solutions that could make things simpler for everyone. Instead of whining and complaining about things that are wrong around here, we have ideas on how to make things better. Besides, we are sick and tired of whining.

M Club women could take credit for a *lot* of everyday things that make life simpler but that we don't even think about anymore. We don't want the credit for suggesting these ideas, which are now in common use, we are just glad we thought of them so life is simpler for a lot of people. Some ideas from M Club women currently enjoyed by all include, but are not limited to, Velcro, paper hankies, wine in a box, squeeze bottles for food products, and the faucet (who do you think was carrying all that water?). M Club women came up with a simple way to hide a *lot* of stuff just lying around too. We built a wall around the stuff and put a door on it and called it *a closet*. It was also our idea to put a handle on *anything*, to attach wheels to anything we might have to carry, and to have carbon copies for checks. You could say that attachments in general were our idea. We invented the lid. We are responsible for the box.

We are currently working on two new ways to make life easier for everyone that are not yet in common use but will soon be. One is the automatic toilet-seat lowering apparatus and the other is the automatic dishwasher-door closer. This is really the same apparatus, the use of which will depend on which way it is installed: right side up or upside down.

Meanwhile, here is another idea we have for making things easier:

"If you are making things too difficult, *stop it*. Please."

M Club Memo

Take this to your doctor's office today!

To: All doctors in these United States

From: The M Club

Re: Scheduling appointments six months in advance

Dear Doctors:

Please make your office personnel stop forcing us make appointments when we leave your office. Make them stop that by 2:00 p.m. EST today, please.

We don't know what we will be doing six months from the time we leave your office. It does not help to give us a little card with a date and time circled. We are sick and tired of little cards and little pieces of paper in general.

Sure, some of us can make it all the way home with the damn little card. We can even find our calendars when we get home. But if it happens to be after June 30, we can't write down our next appointment because nobody buys a calendar for next year in June. We get around to buying the current year's calendar sometime in February.

Even if it is before June 30, there is usually not any room on our calendars anyway. Of course, school is not out until June, so those little boxes on the calendars are already filled up with other appointments. We have appointments for pictures, field trips, community meetings, Girl, Boy, or Cub Scouts, baseball, soccer, ballet, tap dancing, movie dates, and a *lot* of other deadlines. There is no room for a six-months-away doctor's appointment. Sorry.

The M Club has a *better* idea. Why don't we just call your office when we get sick? You would still have plenty of business. You shouldn't worry so much about having appointments six months from now. There will always be people who need you.

We are also sick and tired (mostly tired) of getting charged for an office visit when we miss an appointment because your staff forced us to make one six months ago. We can't even remember the last time we got a haircut, much less an appointment assigned six months ago.

You could really help us out by taking care of this, Doc. In case you don't agree with this simple request, we might start asking you to look at another mysterious spot on our skin that just erupted when we see you out in public. If we run into you getting some movie rentals, eating at a restaurant, on the golf course, and so on (you get the idea), we could use the opportunity for a little consultation. The M Club was responsible for making sure you were not bothered on your time off, but we could rescind that rule quickly. Thanks.

The M Club
Seminars

Teaching is second nature to most M Club members. In our continuing effort to help other people, we teach a *lot* of different kinds of things every day. We are in the habit of teaching.

The M Club holds seminars to teach a wide range of subjects. Look for our seminar announcements in your local newspapers.

We never charge for classes because: (a) education has gotten way too expensive, (b) we don't want to keep track of names on lists of who has paid and who owes because we are sick and tired of keeping track and because we are sick and tired of lists, and (c) we know how to teach.

Some of our seminars include teaching things like:

- How to keep a promise

- How to get a message across with "The M Club Glare"

- How to ask for help

- Words or phrases we believe should be removed from the English language

Our seminars are announced in the newspaper and look like this:

M Club Seminar
October 19, 2004

Bloomington, IN—Join us at IU on a fabulous fall day for a free seminar titled "KISS."

No, goof, Gene Simmons won't be here, although he is certainly welcome to join us.

The KISS seminar is to remind people that every time they kiss a loved one they should repeat to themselves, either silently or aloud, "Keep It Simple Stupid."

We are not sure where this saying came from—maybe it was Lewis Grizzard? Will the originator of this saying please contact TheMClub@aol.com so we may ask permission to use it for our seminar? Thanks.

But we do need to keep it simple, make what we can much simpler. The M Club does not approve of the word "stupid," so the seminar will be called "KIS." You still get the idea.

Let's meet at the pond at IU on October 23. It might be one of those great Indian summer days, and we could simply enjoy the fall day, the touch of wood smoke in the air, the crisp tinge (also in the air), and some crisp apples under a crisp-blue sky. Apple crisp and cider will be served as refreshments. And we can talk about keeping it simple. See you there.

M Club Mandate

The M Club came up with a simple idea and has sent a mandate to a *lot* of companies and all the other folks who want their labels or box tops back in exchange for giving money to schools or for medical research. Here is the form letter we used:

Dear (company president name here):

Thank you so much for giving money to our schools when we turn in soup-can labels, cereal-box tops, lids, receipts, bar codes, little bitty pieces of paper, and lots of other crap.

We appreciate the money you have sent back to our schools. You have sent a *lot* of money back to us. We have bought playground equipment, mats for the gym, flags, paint, caulk, chalk, books, field trips and a lot of other things we needed. Some of you even make donations for medical research. Thank you, again.

The M Club would like to ask a favor. We have proven that we are buying your products, because we have sent your labels, box tops, and codes back to you. We are now in the habit of buying your products. As you know, habits are hard to break. So we will continue to buy your products. We promise.

However, we don't want to keep sending the proof of purchase back to you so you will give us the money for our schools or for badly needed medical research. We think you could give the money *anyway*. It's not like the crap we have been sending back to you is worth anything. After all, it is a lot of old labels and tops you are not going to use again, right?

You will have to trust us to keep buying your stuff. We have trusted all of you for years even after "believe it or not" reports about some pretty weird stuff being found inside your products, the kind of stuff that wasn't supposed to be in there.

So just start sending out that same money you have been sending, except without having to get the garbage back. We can recycle the garbage instead of mailing it back to you. And we can save a lot of time and effort by not collecting all that paper. We have to clean it, save it, organize it, gather it, and mail it. The M Club is in favor of saving time.

Please revise your donation rules by 5:00 p.m. EST today. If you do not agree with this simple request, we will break our habit of buying your stuff from habit. We have broken habits like smoking, cursing, nail-biting, check-bouncing, etc.

(you get the idea). We have helped other people break habits. We can break habits when we want to. And we might start buying products without fancy labels. Nobody wants *those* mailed anywhere. And those cans and boxes have the same things inside.

Again, thanks so much for the help. With all the time we save from not having to collect and mail your labels, we are planning to publish cookbooks using your products as ingredients! We hope you will enjoy the new recipes!

The M Club

M Club Recipes

Cookbooks are so popular these days and are always among the best sellers. We are constantly being bombarded with "new ways," "new styles," or "new attitudes" to cook the same old food. M Club members do not appreciate three-page recipes containing ingredients we cannot find, buy, or pronounce. We keep it simple. We have kept our families and friends alive for many, many years so we must be doing something right. We have really simple recipes because we do not have time to baby-sit food. If we want to massage, caress, sing to, pay hours of attention to, or otherwise make some big deal out of something, we perform all the above on a *person*, not on a food. We just cook food, we don't adopt it. Cook it, serve it, eat it, and move on.

A RECIPE HiSTORY
BROUGHT TO YOU BY THE M CLUB

Did you know it was an M Club member who came up with the recipe for meatloaf? Here's how it happened.

Betty Enderle, a wife and mother of seven children, was sick and tired of making nine hamburgers every time she cooked ground beef, which was about four times a week. She never had been fond of handling raw meat of any kind, even before America found out about that dangerous bacteria that can kill us if we eat it.

One Tuesday, when she was getting ready to cook nine hamburgers, she made up her mind that she would not shape nine little hamburgers anymore, never again, and that is final. She decided to make one big hamburger to save time. The meat was already in the shape of a loaf and she hadn't had any time to loaf for about three years. So she put the meat, already shaped, in a roaster and put it into the oven.

At dinner, the family was surprised. They asked, "What is this new dish, Mom?"

"Meatloaf," Betty said.

With gravy and mashed potatoes, the meatloaf was

very good. Everyone liked it. And Betty got to sit down and have a cup of hot coffee and rest instead of handling raw meat.

On Thursday, the family *asked* for meatloaf again! Betty put some other stuff in this time, like eggs, seasonings, and bread to make it bigger, because two of the kids had brought friends home. It was a hit!

Betty is not the kind of woman who wants credit for figuring out shortcuts to save us time. She is just glad she thought of it so more of her friends could also sit down and have a cup of hot coffee.

In her honor, The M Club is providing Betty's recipe for meatloaf. Here it is:

Betty's Meatloaf Recipe

Put some loaf-shaped ground beef in a roaster.

Mix in anything you think will be good.

Put it in the oven and cook it.

Take it out of the oven when it is done.

Enjoy!

Public Announcement

From: The M Club
February 27, 2005

The M Club has persuaded *all telephone companies* to go back to the way it was, and we want to let you know you will be saving a *lot* of money! You are even getting a rebate!

As you know, the phone companies have been offering too many options to go along with our telephone service, and it looked like they were going to keep adding more and more options. The M Club finally put a stop to all of it. The M Club is sick and tired of too many options. No thanks are necessary, please.

So from now on, forevermore, and this is final, here is the way you use a telephone, in case you didn't know or used to know and somehow forgot:

1. If you hear a ringing sound, pick up the telephone receiver. This will be your signal that someone is calling you and may or may not need to talk to you. However, in case you have recently suffered a blow to the head, this ringing sound may also indicate something else. It is up to you to decide if you are hurt and need to do something about that. *Note:* We will be using the ringing sound *only.* If you hear birds chirping, dogs barking, an

Elvis song, or any other noise, it is *not* the phone anymore.

2. Identify yourself by speaking directly into the part that goes by your mouth. We will not be using the word "hello" anymore. This is a friendly word reserved for people you *want* to talk to. However, The M Club has noticed there are too many people calling who may not be friendly, and you probably don't want to talk to them anyway. Demand identification from the caller immediately. If it is somebody you don't want to talk to, say good-bye and hang up.

3. If you are busy doing something else, let the phone ring. (That could go without saying, but it's very important, so we say it anyway.) The M Club fixed it so that any style of telephone will ring only three times. It will sound like this: *Ring. Ring. Ring.* This will be less stressful for everyone, we believe, and could prevent many accidents, including but not limited to broken toes, middle-aged women running, bathtubs overflowing, etc. (you get the idea). The point here is: If you are not within the three-ring reach rule of the telephone, you don't have to answer it. If it was important, they will call back.

4. Phone locations have changed. Please make sure the appliance is located high up on the wall, at least six feet from floor, and make sure there are no chairs, ladders, or stools in the immediate vicinity. This measure is to prevent anyone under the age of twelve from using the telephone. We thought about issuing permits to use the telephone, but it would take too long and you know how children always say they are older than they are! It is up to adults to make sure it's out of reach. We also thought about putting a child-resistant cap on the receiver end, but that does not work with dangerous medications so we don't think it will work on phones either.

5. Begin using your new phone number today. The M Club has fixed it so we all have only five-digit numbers. Your new phone number is the first five digits of your current number. No more wasted time dialing fifteen numbers! The M Club freed up a *lot* of numbers by shutting down telemarketers, collection agencies, "children's lines," credit-card companies, loan sharks, research companies doing surveys, and *all* automated calling machines. In addition, the cell phone numbers that were being used for "walkie-talkie" purposes have been reassigned. The M Club noticed too many airwaves were being used

to talk to a person within short distances, so
we freed up those too.

6. Phone bills will not exceed $7.50, including
   tax. The M Club *went over there* to all the
   phone companies and had them explain their
   pricing policies. Guess what? They could not
   explain it! So we got them to agree that it
   doesn't really matter who you are talking to
   or where they are, so we should all be charged
   the same amount. This amount is $7.50 per
   month and includes *everything*. Please make
   a note.

7. No more "busy signal." From now on, if you
   hear no voice after three rings, the phone
   automatically disconnects. We are saving a lot
   of time and stress for everyone by doing away
   with the busy signal. Of course, the person
   you are calling may indeed be busy, but we
   don't think it is healthy to keep calling a
   teenager, husband, or best friend for hours
   on end only to hear that annoying signal. For
   this same reason, The M Club wants all the
   redial buttons removed from your phones.
   Use a screwdriver if you want—use whatever
   you want—but get that redial button off your
   phones by 6:00 p.m. EST today. We have only
   five numbers to dial now, and you can just
   dial them. Besides, we kept forgetting *what*

number we dialed last and didn't mean to call *that* person again, so this will save a *lot* of embarrassment. We think you will agree.

8. These services have been discontinued:
   - Call-waiting
   - Caller ID
   - Three-way calling
   - All calls made from or received in the bathroom

   Call-waiting was hurting feelings all over America. Caller ID was redundant because you could find out who was calling by picking up the damn phone. Three-way calling is gone because it is difficult enough to communicate with one person without looking them in the eye. Figure out the last one yourselves.

9. Rebates for the above-mentioned are on the way! The M Club is supervising the rebate program. We got the phone companies to admit that they have collected too much money for years and years. They tried to blame it on "new technology" and "updated services," but we called them on it. Those guys were using the same wires they have always used. The rebate amounts will all be the same. If there is any arguing about your personal rebate amount, you will get *no rebate*.

The M Club is calling this new rebate program "Take It or Leave It Rebate." We suggest
you take it. The amount each of you will get
is $3,213.47.

10. In case we think of any other ways to
straighten this phone company mess out, we
will give you a call. Meanwhile, if you don't
get your rebate by Friday at 10:30 a.m. EST,
please call The M Club and we will go over
there to the phone company again.

Looking forward to your call!

CHAPTER 5

The M Club Means Business Too

"It *is* our business."

The responsibility of dealing with different types of businesses often falls on M Club members. After all, we are an enormous group of consumers and we have some money. We aren't surprised anymore that things we buy from companies fall apart the minute the warranty expires. We aren't even surprised that we get little satisfaction when we fling ourselves onto the customer-service merry-go-round. You know, the ride that begins with a phone call that takes at least an hour to talk to a real person who doesn't really care about your problem, followed by the realization that whatever your problem was it is just too bad. In the end, they always ask us, "Is there anything else I can help you with today?" and we think, "But you haven't helped me with *anything* yet!" It is like a merry-go-round because the entire process makes some of us a little dizzy and a lot of us sick. Sick and tired.

Every corporation has someone at the top. This is the person M Club members want to talk to because this person is able to make decisions that may or may not help us as consumers. Instead of starting at the bottom and working our way up, M Club members start at the top. We are in favor of saving time.

We are also in favor of making things easier. M Club members have that attention to detail along with the common sense to see something for what it is and to clearly see what could make the service or product better. Let's face it, some things have been the same for too long.

For example, as soon as the minivan was introduced, M Club members could see right away that having only one sliding back door on the opposite side of the driver would force M Club drivers with children to walk approximately 2.2 extra miles around the damn van on days when we had two or more errands. If we want to walk 2.2 miles, it would be along a woodland trail or a lake, not around a vehicle. So we "bitched mightily," as Bill Bryson would say, and got the manufacturers to put another door on the other side of the vans.

We also got so sick and tired of our husbands, male friends, sons, fathers (you get the idea) refusing to stop and ask directions that we got navigation systems installed in a lot of newer cars. They wouldn't use a map and they wouldn't ask anyone for directions, so we hinted broadly that a technical gizmo would be *fun* to use, sort of like a video game! "Say, honey, I know we're not *lost,* but wouldn't it be amusing to test this navigation system just to prove you are right about where we are going?" Worked like a charm.

We did the same thing with food products. First, we forced manufacturers to put as many things as they could in squeeze bottles. We told them to put ketchup, mayo, jelly, salad dressings, and the like, into squeeze bottles so we could save time. Then we had to contact them again and make them redesign the bottles so they would be upside down. Apparently, M Club members have to think of everything!

According to M Club research, which is totally made up, we were also responsible for saving 1,536 marriages by seeing to it that the damn toothpaste cap could not be left off of the tube of toothpaste. We made them *attach* the top. We hope consumers also notice our new suggestion of toothpaste with attached tops as well as floss *also* attached to the top. After all, dental care should not take too many steps.

We don't want any credit for making things easier for everyone. We are just glad we thought of these things so people will have more time for the enjoyable things in life, like sitting still for a little while.

M Club Memo

To: Grocery stores that continue to change the "sell by" dates on products

From: The M Club

Re: This means you

The M Club has received too many reports of perishable products that are still being sold after their original expiration date, even after that report on ABC News *20/20* about how they used hidden cameras to catch grocery stores changing the "sell by" dates.

The M Club hereby notifies you stores that the final straw broke the camel's back yesterday. Diane Sawyer got salmonella from some chicken, and she is sick as a dog. Of course, she didn't buy that chicken. She works a lot of hours and doesn't have time to shop. Whoever bought it for her missed Diane's report on *20/20* because she has a few problems of her own and didn't know you stores are still cheating with the dates.

This kind of thing really pisses off The M Club.

You are hereby notified that your stores will be closed. The M Club is *comin' over there* to pack up all that food and give it to *reliable* organizations for immediate distribution. We have boxes. We will pack the food up. We had to pack food for picnics and we have transported large quantities of food from the store to our homes for graduation and birthday parties. We know how to move food.

Your stores will be used as new schools. The lighting is great, and there are all those shelves we will arrange as dividers. We will use the shelves for lots of books and other things the children can keep their things on. It is nice and air-conditioned too—The M Club doesn't think children should be too hot while they are trying to learn how to read.

Gather every single employee of your former store together for a meeting at 4:00 p.m. EST today. Tell them it is *your* fault they have to find another job. Then assign cleaning details for the empty building. We want those floors and shelves to shine! Managers will be assigned to the dirtiest jobs, like cleaning out the freezers. Note: Leave the popsicles for the kids. If you think this is unpleasant, just think of what poor Diane is going through because of your chicken.

I am an attorney for The M Club and I'd get those cleaning supplies gathered up if I were you. These women won't want to wait to see you cleaning after they pack up the food. Most of them have no patience with cheaters anymore.

Camille Doyle
M Club Attorney

P.S. Ammonia and water works just as well as all those other expensive cleaning products. Use what you want, though. Just make sure it *shines*, because the kids will be there Monday.

M Club Invention

*The M Club has ideas
that make good business sense.
We mean business!*

M Club members enjoy many of the conveniences and advantages that new technology has brought to us all. However, some things have become too complicated. We don't pine for "the good old days" (we are *not* very old), but we think a *lot* of things could be simpler. In addition, as fast as technology has advanced, it sometimes has ignored our needs as M Club members. Because we are intelligent, resourceful women who are sick and tired of waiting around for someone else to invent a product or service to suit our needs, we simply invent it ourselves.

This simple invention is the brainchild of our M Club treasurer, Michelle. Michelle is sick and tired of sending her husband, Bob, to the store to get something to feed the family. Bob spends way too much money. Not only that, but out of the 267 separate items Bob brings home there are not any combinations that will make a *meal.*

Michelle appreciates the fact that Bob makes the effort to bring food home. She really does. But Michelle thinks Bob could bring home meal combinations if he steered the shopping cart along the outer walls of the store *only.*

M Club members are not the first to notice that most grocery stores are designed almost the same. We are forced into the vegetable and fruit section upon entering the store. Then a lot of dairy stuff is along another outer wall of the store. Next, the meats are all placed along the back wall. Finally, the breads are put together near the fourth outer wall of the building. Michelle says Bob could do a better job if he didn't stray from the outer walls. If he would not go up and down each aisle, he would get food that made meals and also not spend so much money.

Michelle has invented a sensor to hook onto grocery carts that will sound an alarm if the cart is taken away from the outer wall. In addition, she has designed a special lane, marked on the floor, that will soon be seen in every grocery store in America. The lane looks like a narrow road—you know, with yellow edge lines and a dotted white line down the middle. The men's lane on the floor will go only around the periphery of the store. Michelle put some size 11 footprints inside the lane, painted in orange.

We think Michelle is a genius. Not only will men stick to the outer walls of the store, but they will do the shopping faster. The natural boyish trait of racing the cart through the new lanes will take over, and we think men could be at the checkout with food that will make a meal within six minutes.

So let's all talk to our neighborhood grocery stores about these new inventions. They will be willing to use them because men will have so much fun racing those carts they will go to the store more often and spend money. If these inventions don't work, we will have to come up with some sort of blinders for men to wear at the store so they can't see the aisles with chips and cookies.

It Was No Trouble at All . . .
Because She's My Friend

M Club members are good at taking care of a lot of other people, but sometimes we shy away from demanding satisfaction for ourselves. We go away hurt and bewildered at the treatment we sometimes get, and while we wouldn't think twice about taking up another's cause, we are too sick and tired to make the effort for ourselves.

Nancy didn't ask for help, but was only relating an unfortunate experience that happened to her. Because M Club members are compassionate, we take up for each other without being asked.

"Thank you for calling Wal-Mart. How may I direct your call?" said the department store operator.

"I would like the name of your store manager, please," Jackie said. "And then I would like to be connected with him or her."

"Our store manager is John Goodall but he is not here right now," the operator said. "Would you like to speak to Cathy Johnson, our assistant manager on duty?"

"Yes, and thank you so much for the help," Jackie replied.

"This is Cathy. How can I help you?" the assistant manager said.

"Hi, Cathy, this is Jackie Roth calling. I would like to know how important it is to you if you lose a great big bunch of customers."

"It is very important!" Cathy responded. "What is the problem?"

"Well, my friend Nancy was shopping near your store yesterday when she found one of her tires was flat. She walked all the way across your two-acre parking lot and went to the tire center at your store. She is a member of The M Club, and she is convinced that she can do anything, even though she just had hip-replacement surgery for the second time." Jackie continued, "She probably would have tried to change the damn tire herself, but she thought she would rather pay for some help from your tire department. She walked all the way over there and was told by the tire manager that he was too busy, that she had to have an appointment, that it was just too bad and he could not help her. My friend was over-tired and needed to get home to check on her mother, an Alzheimer's patient, or I am sure she would have taken up for herself. But she didn't. She limped all the way back across the two-acre parking lot, pulled the spare tire and jack out of the car, and was just jacking it up when a kind stranger stopped to help her. *He* didn't want any money or anything. *He* was busy too, having just grabbed some lunch on his half-hour off from his construction job. *He* had the compassion to help my friend. I just thought you might want to know there is someone working for you who not only doesn't want to help other people, he doesn't even want to do his job."

"Give me your friend's name and phone number and I will take care of this," Cathy said.

"The M Club doesn't want him to get fired or anything.

We just won't shop there anymore if we have to put up with this kind of thing," Jackie said.

"I will take care of it," Cathy said.

And she did.

Nancy got a surprise call from Cathy the next day. The tire center gave Nancy a new tire as well as a $50 dollar gift card for anything in the store. When Nancy told her friends about her good fortune, she questioned them to find out who had helped her.

"It must have been a new M Club member," Jackie said. "Cathy took up for you because she might have been in a similar situation herself."

"But she even got that manager to call me and apologize!" Nancy said. "Why do you think she went that extra mile for me? She doesn't even know me!"

"Because she is *in* The M Club and she could," Jackie said.

M Club Seminar
April 17, 2004

Chicago, IL—A new class will be offered at Northwestern University this summer. The M Club is sponsoring the class. There is no registration and the class is free. "The History and Effective Use of the Hissy Fit" will be taught from 10:00 a.m. to 4:00 p.m. EST on June 3, 2004.

Syllabus:

10:00 a.m. EST: Students will learn the origin of the hissy fit. The M Club believes the first recorded hissy fit was thrown when a woman had tried everything she knew to straighten out some kind of consumer issue and, as a last resort, was forced to make use of this secret weapon.

11:00 a.m. EST: A short break. Strong, hot coffee provided free of charge.

11:15 a.m. EST: The class will continue with a discussion on "The Effective Use of the Hissy Fit." In case students didn't know or used to know but somehow forgot, the hissy fit should be reserved for the time when other methods of getting a message across have failed. Other methods, in order of their proposed appearance, are:

1. The M Club Glare
2. Heavy sighing with eyes looking upward
3. Heavy sighing with eyes filled to the brim with tears (tears must not overflow brim at this time, which takes some practice)
4. Repeat statement of your position in an even tone using steps 1–3 simultaneously
5. Permission granted to throw hissy fit.

Students will see that throwing a hissy fit is a *process*. Students will find out that overuse of the hissy fit without proper preceding steps is less effective overall, because sometimes the hissy fit could be saved on account of a previous step resulting in the desired outcome.

12:00 p.m. EST: Catered lunch provided by The M Club.

1:00 p.m. EST: The group will watch several senior M Club members demonstrate the five steps of throwing an effective hissy fit. M Club instructors have perfected the tool, so this shouldn't take long.

1:15–2:00 p.m. EST: Students will practice the five steps to an effective hissy fit while M Club instructors make helpful suggestions.

2:00 p.m. EST: Short break for strong, hot coffee and homemade macaroons (Debi's special recipe).

2:15 p.m. EST: Discussion of actual events that recently inspired hissy fits. Discussion of actual events that *should* have inspired a hissy fit but did not because we were too tired. Discussion of possible effects of the overuse of hissy fits.

2:30–4:00 p.m. EST: Students will break into small groups. "Hissy fit" throwing disks (plastic saucer-shaped items embossed with the words "Hissy Fit") will be distributed. Students will throw these hissy fits until they are comfortable with their own hissy-throwing accuracy.

Meet by the pond at Northwestern. Don't be afraid to approach the group already there. They are just *practicing* their hissy fits. See you there!

M Club Invention

The M Club wants the manufacturers of washing machines to know that we are the ones who spend time with their machines, mostly. Some of us spend time with them in nice, organized laundry centers, but most of us spend time with those machines in the basement. Maybe those companies haven't ever seen a basement in an old American house. Maybe if they did they would understand why we don't want to spend a *lot* of time down there with those machines. So The M Club has come up with a new invention. We think those companies should get busy and make some laundry chutes to attach to the top of *every* washing machine from now on, forevermore, and that is final. Here is the description: We want some kind of flexible chute that clamps onto the top of the washer. It should be long enough to reach to the second floor of our homes. The chute could be constructed so it accommodates off-chutes, which we will attach to our kid's bedrooms and bathrooms.

Then, we want them to figure out some kind of voice command to start the machine. When we look down the chute and see the washer is full, we want to shout down the chute and say, "Wash that!" Maybe we could call our new invention "Shout Down the Chute."

We don't care what they call it, but we want something figured out by Friday at 8:00 a.m. EST. It *must* be a *free* option on those new machines. We are sick and tired of all those options being so expensive. We don't want to tell the machines the specific content of each article of clothing anymore either. The machine should just wet the clothes, swish them with soap, and spin them. That's all.

Guess what? We will be washing a lot more clothes with the help of the chutes, and the washing machine motors will wear out faster and we will have to buy more washers. As you can see, our invention makes good business sense! We hope a *lot* of washing machines with our invention attached will be on the market very soon. Or else The M Club will have to *go over there.*

M Club Letter

February 28, 2004
Hinney-Walker Funeral Home
Att: Director Jeff Verbus

Director Verbus:

Please hire some new advertising agency to get out a new print ad for your funeral-home business by 5:00

p.m. EST on Monday. Meanwhile, The M Club wants you to call the newspapers that are running your current ad and cancel it. Do it by 2:30 p.m. EST today please.

The ads are probably not working very well anyway, so you may as well start over. Jeff, The M Club does not believe there are *any* funeral homes that can advertise "Remembrance Without Regrets." This is a contradictory phrase if we ever heard one!

When M Club members have been forced to use the services of a business like yours, *we always have regrets.* How can you not understand this, Jeff? We don't care how old the person we are making arrangements for was. There have always been and there will always be regrets.

It does not matter what the situation was. We may have spent a *lot* of time or a little time with this person; we may have gotten along or not; we may have given everything or nothing to this person; we might have tried our best or not at all. The point is that there are always regrets and you must not give the impression by your advertisement that anything else is true. It is not true.

Jeff, in case you didn't know, we all do the best we can with the resources available at the time. And when it is time to "make arrangements" for a loved one, we do not want to hear we could have done better and we should have no regrets.

Don't you run that ad again, Jeff, or you might regret it.

If the M Club sees one more printed ad from your business with that phrase, we are comin' over there. Our Club has about forty million members in America alone. We are the ones who make "arrangements" a *lot*. And we will make some "arrangements" for you if you don't pull that ad.

M Club members would be happy to help you find a new advertising agency or help you come up with a new ad for your business. We are creative and we have computers. Contact us at TheMClub@aol.com.

Thanks for taking care of this, Jeff. See you soon.

The M Club

M Club Invention

Dee Spears, M Club member since 2003, relates the circumstances surrounding her new M Club invention. Dee explains:

My vacuum cleaner sucks. Well, that is a misnomer because the one I got does not suck, actually. My husband bought me one of those Dirt Devils "with new swivel glide and featuring seven carpet height adjustments" for my birthday in September. I got a red one because he knows I like roses. Anyway, I have only had it a couple of months and it will not suck anymore.

I lost the little book that came with the thing, but I have taken vacuum cleaners apart before. I *know* sometimes it is a belt problem. So I got a Phillips head screwdriver and turned the thing upside down (after I unplugged it, of course). There are handy directions on the bottom of the machine for all those M Club members who also lost the little book. The directions said: "Remove four screws near nozzle to check belt." In case you didn't know, there is no nozzle on the underneath side of the machine!

So I just removed all the screws that I could find.

Things were going very well until my husband came in just then. He pulled the assembly apart and helped me inspect the belt, which appeared to be in good working order. Before I could stop him, he proceeded to take the screws out of the motor cover. Of course, I *know* that if it is a motor problem there is nothing I can do about it, and that looking under there is a great big waste of time. When I said as much to my husband, he dropped the screwdriver and walked away. I was able to resume my repairs on the machine.

I had already checked the bag as well as the filters. I had already reamed all the hoses to make sure there weren't any clogs (German shepherds sure shed a *lot!*). I used a shish-kebab skewer for this. When I got it all put back together, it still would not suck.

I, for one, appreciate the low price on those Dirt Devil vacuums. I looked at the thing and decided it would be worth $89.95 to me just to throttle the thing, and if I broke it I would just buy a new one. Guess what? It worked!

So here is a new invention to improve vacuum cleaners:

1. New vacuums will *all* include some eighteen-inch shish-kebab skewers.
2. Those unclear directions will be taken off of the bottom of the machines.
3. The motor casing has been sealed.
4. *Simpler* instructions for users are now *attached* to the machine. We used a sturdy, laminated card that says: "WHEN USER HAS TRIED EVERYTHING ELSE, THROTTLING MACHINE SOMETIMES WORKS."

Instructions for throttling appliance:

1. Grip handle firmly and bang on floor.
2. Now bang against sturdy, immovable object using a side-to-side motion.
3. Repeat.
4. Turn vacuum upside down.
5. Throttle again.

6. Throttle once more in right-side-up position.

7. If it still won't suck, use a broom.

8. E-mail TheMClub@aol.com and we will make sure the company sends you a check by 6:00 p.m. EST. (We will make them wire the money to you.)

M Club Letter

March 15, 2004
Western Union
Att: Jack Ferndale, CEO

Hi, Jack,

Please make sure your money-wiring systems are at peak performance today by 5:00 p.m. EST. The M Club is sending a *lot* of business your way!

You see, Jack, The M Club is sick and tired of waiting around for people who owe us money to get it to us. We do not want to wait "six to eight weeks" for the money a big corporation is supposed to send us so we can go buy another product to replace the one we just bought.

The M Club began our new campaign with Scott Baaske over there at the Dirt Devil vacuum cleaner place. He might be calling you to wire a *lot* of money, and we want Western Union to be ready. Make sure you have plenty of insulation on your wires, because The M Club has fixed it so that those wires will be *burning up* with money transfers!

Meanwhile, if you have been planning a system-wide upgrade of any kind, put those plans into effect now too. The M Club will also be demanding that many other companies use your money-wiring services. We are contacting car manufacturers, CD-player makers, lots of "roadside assistance" companies, credit-card folks, universities, Mr. Coffee, and so on. This is only a partial list, but you get the idea.

So get those wires warmed up, or whatever you do over there to get ready for a *lot* of companies to wire a *lot* of money. It is not necessary to thank The M Club for bringing you so much new business, Jack. We don't do things because we expect thanks. We simply expect things to get done more quickly, because we are forty million women who just don't have much patience with waiting anymore.

Looking forward to your faster wiring system by next week!

The M Club

M Club Memo

To: Pharmaceutical companies
From: The M Club
Re: Commercials that ask questions

Those questions are really stupid. Why are you asking if we worry? Why do you want to know if we feel anxiety? Why do you say a chemical imbalance is to blame?

We have some questions for you. How can your drug make us not worry about terrorists? Why are you blaming our own brains? When did the God-given, fight-or-flight response become a human instinct that needs to be treated with your expensive drug?

You are also spending too much money on advertising. And you are spending too much money giving away samples of your drug to every doctor in America.

The M Club is hereby notifying you that your commercials and print ads will stop effective August 30, 2004, at 1:00 p.m. EST. You pharmaceutical companies sure pulled those ads on hormone replacement therapy drugs in the blink of an eye when the National Institutes of Health came out with their study on July 2, 2002. They said your HRT drugs were dangerous and that the risks outweigh the benefits.

So pull the other ads now.

Don't give us that crap about waiting until after September 11 to pull the ads. Your drugs will not help us get through the anniversary of that horrific day. We will lean on each other. We will feel fear again. We will feel anxiety. We will be damn depressed. We will worry again. There is nothing you can do about this. We will get through it somehow. God will help us.

With all the money you save from the ads, we want you to *lower the prices* of *all* your other drugs. Slash those prices. Blue light those suckers. Make those prices so low they think they are a snake's belly in a wagon track. Do it today.

Or you will get a little visit from The M Club. How does that make you feel? Does it make you worry? Does that cause you anxiety? Might you lose sleep over the thought of us coming over there?

It should.

M Club Letter

February 2, 2004
Sony Corporation of America
Att: Howard Stringer, Chairman and
     Chief Executive Officer

Hi, Howard,

I wanted to let you know my new CD player was working great until the wire from one of the headphones came loose. Now I have to sit with one hand up to my ear to hold the damn wire. I look like I'm thinking hard about some big problem. Howard, the point of using headphones with my CD players is to listen to music and *not* think.

I'll bet a lot of people who have one of these expensive sets have had this happen to them when it was still relatively new. We don't have our receipts because we are sick and tired of keeping track of little pieces of paper.

Howard, on behalf of all the other customers who are listening to music during their relaxation time and holding one or both hands on their ears so they can hear the damn music, we want you to send new CD players with *better* headphones to every hospital in America.

There are millions of us, Howie, and your company is saving a lot of money by not having to replace those headphones because we can't return them without the receipt.

Think of it this way: The CD players don't cost you as much as you sell them for, and you offer them for free to companies as incentives to people who probably already have CD players. So just start shipping them out to all the hospitals. The patients there don't have CD players and could use some music to help make them feel better.

Send batteries with the CD players, Howard. Send a lot of batteries for each player, because your CD players are made to eat up batteries like they were going out of style!

If my local hospital doesn't receive CD players by next week, The M Club will find all those receipts and you could be facing bankruptcy when we return all those junky headphones. We will not exchange; we will return. It could cause quite an upset in your financial department.

So start getting those CD players shipped out. No, we will not tell you which hospitals we are going to check. You had better send them to *all* the hospitals. Get them shipped now so the patients will have them on Valentine's Day. Lots of them will be thinking of loved ones they can't be with on that "day of love," and they should have a surprise gift.

Thanks for taking care of this, Howard.

M Club President

M Club Invention

M Club members will be happy to know that manufacturers are taking our suggestion and will now make most of their irons in brighter colors with lots of logos and stuff on the sides and handles. We told them to look at some skateboards or something and copy those designs.

We think men and boys will be very attracted to the new designs and even pick up the irons to see what they are. We are willing to help with the sales effort by explaining that an iron is an appliance that heats up and smoothes wrinkles out of clothes.

The new irons we ordered include an indestructible card (*attached*) with instructions for using the appliance. Here is what the instruction card says:

M CLUB INSTRUCTIONS FOR USE:

1. PLUG IT IN.
2. TURN IT ON.
3. WHEN IT GETS HOT, PUT IT ON WRINKLES.
4. WHEN YOU THINK ENOUGH WRINKLES ARE GONE, TURN IT OFF.
5. UNPLUG IT.

The M Club's new invention also has eliminated so many choices for heat setting and fabric selections. Our new flashy logo irons go "on" or "off." We were sick and tired of having to figure out *what* we are trying to iron instead of just ironing it. Ours just *gets hot.*

Watch your newspaper for our new press campaign, which we designed to sell our invention. It is a clever one and could change American fashion overnight. We call it "The M Club Has Wrinkles and So Do You."

M Club Letter

Nike World Headquarters

Att: Philip H. Knight, CEO, President, and Chairman, Nike Inc.

CC: The five new vice presidents appointed August 27, 2003: Tom Arndorfer, Vice President and Chief Financial Officer of Nike USA; Jim Carter, Vice President, General Counsel; Adam Helfant, Vice President of U.S. Sports Marketing; John Hoke, Vice President, Global Footwear Design; and Bernie Pliska, Vice President, Corporate Controller.

Hi, guys, and congrats on your new jobs!

We think it is a fine saying you came up with for your company to get recognition. "Just Do It" is short and sweet and gets the message across with an economy of words. The M Club believes that is the best way to get a message across.

Even John Wayne is quoted as once saying, "Talk low. Talk slow. And don't talk too much."

We agree.

However, The M Club would like to point out that we used that phrase first. We, all of us, issued orders to lots of people for years—for example, "Clean your room," "Stop that!" "Go get the mail, please," "Be home by 11:00 p.m. EST," and many others. You get the idea.

Anyway, then we always had to say, "Just do it." Even though most of the people we issued the orders to had perfect hearing, we had to use the phrase too.

It is fine that you use the phrase. We like the message of encouragement you are trying to give. But The M Club wants you to give encouragement in other ways too. Stop giving all that spokesperson money to just one person. We know he or she is great. But there are lots of other people trying as hard as they can at the sports of tennis, golf, football, baseball, and basketball. If you are sponsoring anyone in the sport of cricket, please include them too.

We want you to spread that money out *evenly* among *all* the players. Just divide those billions by the total number of players and you will get the amount that everyone should receive. We don't think that will be too hard, because M Club members can still do long division, by hand, without a calculator. So *just do it*. Do it today by 4:30 p.m. EST.

These are only games anyway, you know. And nothing promotes sportsmanship like everybody being treated fairly, now does it?

We think the money you send to *all* the kids will come in handy. Some could finally say, "Gee, Dad, I don't want to play anymore. I want to raise German shepherds for blind people."

After all, this is America and people are allowed to do whatever they want. Within reason, of course.

Sincerely,
Kathryn Sultzbaugh, M Club President
Five vice-presidents of The M Club:
Cindy Marie Lyons, M Club Vice President since 2003
Jenn Bradfield, M Club Vice President
Alice Springowski, M Club Vice President
Gloria Behm, M Club VIP
Nancy Hockenberry, M Club Vice President

M Club Memo

To: All refuse and garbage disposal companies in the U.S.
From: The M Club
Attn: CEOs

Please go buy some more garbage trucks. Do it today. Do it by 9:00 p.m. EST, because beginning tomorrow there will be a *lot* more garbage for you to pick up on your regular routes.

This will mostly be paper from a couple of million new *excuse deposit receptacles*. These receptacles aren't really new. They used to be suggestion boxes, but nobody was taking our suggestions so they are being used for a *better* purpose now. We think you will agree that it is high time somebody started collecting and disposing of all the excuses around here. The M Club doesn't want any thanks. We just want *you* to collect them, because you are already collecting all that other trash.

Please make sure your men don't leave any excuses lying around on the floor when they collect those excuses. Make sure no excuses blow out of those trucks too. We do *not* want to see anyone finding any old excuse and using it.

It is up to you all to burn those excuses or bury them or whatever you do with all the other garbage. Don't recycle them, though. The M Club is sick and tired of recycled excuses. Just get rid of them.

In addition, make sure those new trucks you buy are big enough. You may be hauling around some *big excuses*, and it is up to you to transport them. If any of your workers make a move toward stealing any of those old excuses, please notify The M Club immediately by e-mail. Send those names to TheMClub@aol.com and we will *come over there* and deal with those guys ourselves.

Thanks for the help! See you soon!

M Club Invention

The M Club has invented a new type of computer keyboard! The delete key on all new computers coming out, from now on, forevermore, will be a *lot* bigger.

We also made the delete key red.

We were sick and tired of signing onto our private computer internet connection every day and finding e-mail from people we don't know. We don't even *want* to know them.

Debi Rice, M Club member since 2003, also wanted to

put a stop to all those flashing ads. All of them. She was sick and tired of getting dizzy when she tried to read her computer screen.

Those companies that can't afford to have a website without advertising will have to save some money and come back on the internet when they have it. They should pay for their own websites anyway, instead of making someone else pay for it.

So our M Club keyboard comes with a hammer. The hammer is *attached* to the keyboard for convenience and ease of use. Look for our invention in stores near you very soon. If consumers see any of our inventions with a bigger delete key in any color other than red, please notify TheMClub@aol.com. If it has a blue or green delete key, it is not ours. We are sick and tired of too many choices around here.

M Club Letter

March 21, 2004
Colgate-Palmolive Company
Att: Reuben Mark, Chairman of the Board
      and Chief Executive Officer

Hi, Reuben:
We like your dish soap. We don't even mind all the commercials you spend so much money on for a product

that everyone needs and would buy anyway without the advertising.

The M Club, however, thinks you should stop hiring all those young, young women to be in your commercials and ads. We want *boys* and *men* in your commercials from now on.

Furthermore, don't go back to that damn commercial about how good your soap is for our hands. We don't care about our hands. We have given our own good gloves to our children to keep their hands warm because they wouldn't keep track of their own gloves.

So just get some *males*, young ones and old ones, and start putting them in your commercials. We want to see them washing a *sinkload* of dishes. Glasses first, then silverware, then dishes, then pots and pans. It is up to you to teach the correct way to wash dishes, because you are spending too much money on commercials.

Put the directions on the back of the bottles too. Why do you have instructions that read "Put soap in water and swish"? We know how to use soap. We just don't want to use it anymore, because we are sick and tired of washing dishes.

If we don't see some *males,* old ones and young ones, in your commercials by next week, The M Club will have Hotpoint deliver new dishwashers to every woman in the country who doesn't have one and is forced to use your stupid soap. They manufacture dishwashers that leak on wooden kitchen floors the minute the warranty expires, and The M Club has already taken care of that little problem.

Looking forward to those new ads next week!

Rose Bloom
M Club member since '03

P.S. Start with male teenagers. Do *not* hire a model. Regular kids have to wash dishes too.

M Club Mission

We're going over there!

M Club members are invited to our M Club field trip to Carpets-R-Us in Evansville, Indiana.

We are *going over there* because the requested changes in the way carpeting is measured have not been made. The M Club requested that they *stop* measuring carpeting in square inches or square feet or square yards. After all, we have enough to figure out without having to strain our brains multiplying and dividing numbers to come up with how much it will cost to carpet a damn room. We have had to figure out what to make for dinner 365 days a year for twenty-five years. We don't want to figure out carpet measurements. We want *carpet sellers* to figure it out, and to put the damn price on the room-size rugs, including the tax.

Also, The M Club politely requested that they start selling carpeting for all one price. Carpeting is carpeting. We were sick and tired of the excuse about this one being more expensive than that one because of the color or the swirls or the thickness. It cost just about as much to make it, so we wanted them to stop charging different prices for every single one.

What to bring on the field trip: Bring children with muddy shoes. In case M Club members don't have children, borrow some. Make sure the shoes are *really* muddy. We will break one of our cardinal rules about kids not walking on new carpeting with muddy shoes and allow them to walk on all the new carpeting they have over there. And they will do it, too, because no matter how many times we used to tell them not to, they still walked on our new carpets. Kids are darling, don't you think?

We hope our M Club field trip will demonstrate to the company president that M Club members mean business, and that *we mean what we say*. Hope you can join us.

M Club Letter

Kenmore Appliances
Cc: Hotpoint, Whirlpool, and all stove companies
   in America

Dear CEOs:

The M Club likes your products. Mostly. But we have a few suggestions for you all. We are the ones who pick out and buy the stoves, and we are the ones to cook on them, mostly. So we hope you will consider the following suggestions:

It is time for a redesign. After all, your stoves have been the same since you first came out with them. We are talking about the size of the burners. Why do you keep making only one big burner and three small crappy burners on every stove?

The M Club has a better idea. Enclosed please find the designs drawn by our talented and real women who actually cook on your stoves.

You will notice that there is only one small crappy burner now. We hardly need small burners anymore because we can microwave the vegetables and other things we used to cook in small pans on the stove.

Please note there are three big burners: one for our grandmother's cast-iron skillet, one for a wok, and one for those of us who process our garden produce in great big canners. You might have watched your own wives try to can tomatoes and seen with your own eyes that the damn stovetop wasn't close to being big enough and that the burners were very inadequate.

Also, we want the ovens to *all* be self-cleaning, from now on. We do not mean that drips just stay there as long as it takes to burn up, days and sometimes weeks after the drippage occurred. Stop calling those "self-cleaning." Figure out a real self-cleaning oven. We want the ideas for a *real* self-cleaning oven by Friday at 5 p.m. EST. Note: Don't try to use that "turn oven to 700 degrees to clean oven" crap. We don't like it *that* hot in our kitchens.

Don't forget to notice that the enclosed new burner designs have entirely omitted those stupid rings and drip pans around and under the burners. We want those areas to be self-cleaning too. They are disgusting. Figure something out by Friday.

Looking forward to your new lines this fall!

The M Club

M Club Letter

September 22, 2004
Nextel Corporation
Att: John Kropf

Dear Mr. Kropf:
We are happy for you because your phones are sure being used a *lot*. We definitely approve of ingenuity that makes it possible for people to reach each other any time it's necessary.

However, we think the walkie-talkie thing is going too far. A lot of people are using walkie-talkies when they really don't need to. We have seen a husband and wife use them within arm's length of each other. For some reason, they feel the need to report every step of their location until they meet up. This is silly.

Maybe these people didn't have walkie-talkies when they were little. We don't know. Maybe these people have become unable to be alone and quiet for a while. We don't know that either.

Please turn off the airwaves, or whatever you do, and stop them before they lose the ability to *look* for someone they are meeting. Turn those off so others can *listen* to some birdsong or rustling leaves instead of static. There is nothing wrong with *calling* to another using a *voice* instead of a walkie-talkie.

We are counting on you to fix this noisy problem by noon EST today. If you won't, we might reach out and touch someone, and it might be you.

Thanks.

The M Club

M CLUB MANUAL INSTRUCTIONS

In our continuing effort to teach others how to handle situations, The M Club is providing instructions on "How to Write an Effective Letter of Complaint." Use the one below as an outline, or purchase our M Club stationery to take care of some M Club business of your own.

Our stationery comes in a variety of wine-colored backgrounds. The M Club does not approve of excessive whining, so choose whichever wine color you need for your specific purpose. Write your complaint letter on burgundy-colored paper if your complaint is of a full-bodied, strong, and whiney nature. Or use rose-colored paper for your moderately whiney complaints. Complaints in a lighter vein could be classified as annoyances rather than actual whiney complaints, so use Chablis-colored paper with a lighter texture.

The M Club has had great success with this form letter, and we hope you do too. If you mean business like we mean business, use this business letter format. As always, if you don't receive immediate satisfaction from your M Club complaint letter, simply e-mail M Club headquarters at TheMClub@aol.com. We will be happy to help!

Form Letter to Get Action

Instructions: Fill in the blanks

Date:
Company Name:
Company Address:
Name of Head of Company:

Do *not* address "customer service." They *cannot* help you. It is up to you to find out who is *in charge*. And do *not* use "Dear" when addressing this person.

(First graph:) *Tell them what you want,* here in the first graph. Be specific.

(Second graph:) *State your complaint* here in the second graph. Cut to the chase. Be blunt yet polite.

(Third graph:) The **M Club** is granting permission to use its name in a *nonviolent threat only,* so tell them *we will all come over there* to have a little chat if your problem is not resolved to your satisfaction immediately. (We can get someone there within the hour. We have a lot of members. Have a cup of hot coffee while you wait for the others. Sit down. They will be there shortly.)

Now sign your name. Just sign your name. Leave out "All the best" unless you really mean it. Do not use

"Sincerely"; your message itself should make the impression that you *sincerely* mean what you say. Don't use "Cordially," either. You cannot be pissed off and cordial at the same time.

Note: The M Club believes in you, ladies. You can take care of many problems using this simple form-letter approach. You can do it. If immediate resolution is not forthcoming, e-mail TheMClub@aol.com. We will be right there.

CHAPTER 6

The Media

Can you believe there are a *lot* of people around here who think everything they hear on the news or see in print is actually true? M Club members have lived long enough to know we must consider media reports with the utmost care and decide for ourselves whether or not to believe them.

The M Club is sick and tired of media reports that are followed by additional information reported days or weeks or years later that totally contradicts the first report. We are sick and tired of contradictions.

We are also sick and tired of the new trend of "reality television." M Club members used to watch television so we could relax and *not* think about reality. The reason the media must make some changes is that there are a *lot* of people who are influenced by things they see in print or see and hear on television.

In addition, The M Club thinks it is high time the media took their responsibilities more seriously. Those guys know they are influencing a *lot* of people.

Here are some of our M Club ideas concerning changes we would like to see in the media. These are mostly in the form of a standard "press release" because those media people are used to getting their messages this way; it is a format they can understand. You wouldn't talk to a kid in a language he or she doesn't understand (like English), would you? So The M Club uses the language of the media, which is *the press release.*

Of course, the media's job is to find news to put in the papers, on television, in magazines, on the internet, and so on. A press release is just one way of notifying people in the media that if they want the scoop, they could put it in their papers, magazines, internet articles, or on television. The M Club uses press releases as well as "public announcements," and sometimes individual letters to the person or persons who may be able to help.

M Club Letter

August 3, 2004
Charlie Gibson, c/o ABC News

Dear Charlie,

We know it was not your fault that you showed the rerun of that report on lying, but The M Club is upset because you and your colleagues interviewed the wrong experts for the piece.

The experts said that everybody lies all of the time. They quoted such statistics as "twenty-five lies per day per person" and "lying begins at a young age, as early as three years old."

Charlie, we have been working hard for a long time to curb lying, and we thought we were making headway. We know we have made advances, and now you are telling everyone we haven't accomplished anything.

First of all, the test they set up to see if the little kids would lie were flawed. You should have had the child's mother tell her child not to turn around and look at the toy while she was out of the room, and then have her come back in and ask the kid if he had looked. All our kids would have said, "No, ma'am." And they wouldn't have lied. You should not have used that other woman to perform that test. I wouldn't do what she told me either. Her voice was very annoying and too singsongy. Kids don't like to be talked to like that.

Second, the other test you showed, when Diane made the nasty chili and invited seven of her friends over for lunch, was flawed too. It was a setup to see if any of her friends would lie to her about the chili she fixed for them.

The M Club is really pissed off about that one. We took up for Diane when we thought it was the old chicken that made her sick. We closed some grocery stores and made them into new schools and everything. Now we suspect that Diane got sick as a dog from that chili—which is her own fault, trying to fool her friends like that. Did anyone else get sick? We can't even *say* "anchovy paste" without gagging. Diane shouldn't have put that in there.

Well, Charlie, The M Club wants you to find some *better* experts and do another report on lying. We have spent a *lot* of time and threats teaching other people not to lie. And now you say everybody does it and it looks like it is okay to lie. Please don't encourage that kind of thing. And don't show that rerun again either.

M Club members would be happy to be interviewed as experts on your new report, "Our Other Lying Report Was a Big Lie." Give us a call.

The M Club

M Club Letter

August 4, 2004
Garth Brooks
c/o Capitol Records

Hi Garth,

We love you. We love your songs. But in case you are planning to come out of retirement (who doesn't?), we want you to stop singing "Shameless." Please don't sing it again.

The M Club has been telling other people for years and years that they *should* be ashamed when they do something they know in their hearts was wrong. Sometimes it was the only threat we could come up with. We used it a *lot.*

But your song says that *you* are "shameless," and it might be undoing all those "I am ashamed of you" threats we have used for years. And years. We are sick and tired of doing our work over again.

Garth, you are influencing a lot of people. We saw how many people showed up for your concert in Central Park a few years ago. We saw you on that Navy ship too. Those boys really need to know you do not think *anyone* is shameless.

So please stop singing "Shameless." The music is fine. Just go back into the studio and re-record it without the words. Or make up some other words to go with the music. We don't care which you do, but we want it done by Saturday.

Thanks, Garth. Keep up the good work!

The M Club

P.S. Please let Billy Joel know we don't want him singing it anymore either. We know it was his song first, but you made it a hit, so it is up to you to let him know. Thanks.

Public Announcement

American students at American schools anywhere in America will not have to bring their own paper to school anymore. The M Club has arranged for tons and tons of paper to be delivered to your schools for *free.*

Where did we get all this paper, you ask?

We have finally shut down all those trashy newspaper tabloids you used to see near the checkout at supermarkets. They were using too much paper for despicable purposes, and we finally put them out of business.

How, you ask?

It was really a stroke of genius, in our opinion. As you

know, The M Club has millions of members now. We, all of us, reached under the cushions of the couch and took the change from there. Some of us saved the change from the pockets of dirty clothes nobody empties. Others reached under the seats of the car. We pooled all this money together, and—here's the good part—*we bought up the ink companies that supply the tabloids.*

Is this genius?

We put our most polite members on the phone banks, and when the tabloid companies called to order more ink, we said, "We are out of ink. Call back next week." They did, and we kept repeating the line, and pretty soon they ran out of ink! No ink, no tabloid.

They were quite furious, as you can imagine. But we waited a while and then had the same girls call to say we would take all that blank paper off their hands. For a small fee. We have a *lot* of paper now, and we have already started sending it out to the schools.

The money the tabloids paid us to take the paper off their hands will be used to create a lap-size newspaper, *Good News Is Everywhere.* People will smile when they read this paper. It will be written and edited by members of The M Club. Helen Thomas is in charge.

No thanks are necessary. M Club members have had to deal with a *lot* of paper over the years. We know what to do with paper. Look for your free school paper coming to a school near you very soon!

For sale: Ink. Lots of it. Four colors.

Inquire at TheMClub@aol.com. For sale to artists only, and we check credentials.

M Club Mission

The M Club has plans in the works to *go over there* to all the movie studios, including but not limited to Paramount, Metro-Goldwyn-Mayer, and all movie studios except Disney.

We will be visiting with the presidents, CEOs, and those other fellows in charge of making movies. We will tell them that we like a lot of their movies. We laugh. We cry. We cringe. We remember them.

But we want them to stop making so many awfully violent movies. They should stop now. Why are they disregarding the researched fact that seeing violence all the time is not good for people? Everyone knows that.

"We are producers and directors ourselves," we will say. "We have produced the children who are being harmed by your violent movies. We have directed everything from behind the scenes for most of our lives. We are good at directing. We direct traffic, family members, music, meal-making, and shoe-buying for other people."

"We can produce and direct *better* movies," we will say in unison. "We suggest you look for some better scripts. Look in new books. Don't tell us you can't find any. Look for them!"

M Club members who choose to attend the movie field trip should meet by the pond in Studio City. Please be prepared to *go over there* to Disney, just in case. Those folks are cutting it close sometimes. Sexual innuendoes don't go over every child's head like they think. We will ask them to tighten those reins on Mickey.

M Club Letter

August 11, 2004
Phil McGraw, c/o NBC

Hi Phil,

You made a great big mistake on a recent show, so you will have to get those guests back, arrange for the same audience to come back, and do the show over. Don't tell us you can't find the audience members. Look them up! They were the people who sat there while you yelled at those women who gave gifts to other people and you told them they were *wrong*.

Phil, Phil, Phil! You are extremely fortunate that an M Club member was not in attendance that day. We are busy taking care of a *lot* of other things around here.

To recap: You made a show about women who give a *lot* of things to other people, and you told them they were selfish. You said they gave for the wrong reasons. Then you convinced them that they even expected something back just because they gave to someone. One lady even brought gifts to you and your staff because you had all been so nice to her. She brought a framed print for you and your wife. You proceeded to take all the gifts out of the bag and criticize each one. Then you said you would not accept them.

"My staff is nice to people because I pay them to be nice," you said to your guest. Then you said she could not give your staff the small thank-you gifts she had brought for them. You are lucky our M Club president did not witness this cruelty in person. Even though The M Club has a strict policy of nonviolence, our own M Club president was so incensed that she might have gotten up out of the audience and snatched you bald-headed if you weren't already that way.

You see, Phil, The M Club's forty million members have been working for a long time trying to teach others that giving is a *good* thing. We show people how to give from the heart, we give examples, give until it hurts, give time and attention, and give our all to help other people. Because of that one show, we are afraid some people got the wrong impression and now think giving is wrong just because you said so. We are sick and tired of doing our work over again, Phil.

The M Club wants you to do that show over. Re-tape that show by Monday, November 1, 2004, at 5:00 p.m. EST. It is up to you to figure out what time the new show will air in all the other time zones in the United States. We want you to promote the replacement show with commercials and print advertising, which you will have to pay for yourself. The message should be: "I was wrong. Giving is never wrong, no matter for what reason the giving was accomplished. I was wrong. Be sure and watch my show on Monday, November 1, 2004, at 5:00 p.m. EST and I will tell you all why I was wrong!"

Then you will have to outline at least ten good points to explain why it really doesn't matter *why* or *what* or *how* or *when* or *who* this giving was done to or for. The act of giving, in itself, is never wrong, like you were. Please send your ten-good-points outline to The M Club at our e-mail address by Friday, August 13, 2004, at 1:00 p.m. EST. Send the outline to TheMClub@aol.com. We will give you an idea if you are on the right track because we are a giving group. Don't tell us you can't come up with ten good points on giving. Think of some!

You will also have to use the weekend to go shopping and *buy gifts* for those women who you convinced were selfish for giving because it made them feel good or convinced they were giving for the wrong reason. Please make sure you put some *thought* into the gifts you get for them too, the way they put *thought* into the gifts they give to others. Of course, you will have to find out a little more about them as individuals before you can give them something they can use. Don't try giving them back the same gifts they brought for you though, Phil. If you try that, we are fairly sure The M Club President will *come over there* herself, and this whole thing has upset her so much that you really don't want that to happen.

Well, Phil, you have a busy couple of days coming up, so you should get busy. Looking forward to those ads and the new show on Monday!

The M Club

P.S. Because we are so giving, we are giving you a break this time. However, don't let it happen again or *we will all come over there.* You will need a much bigger studio because we have forty million members. If we have to *come over there,* Sara says to make sure there are enough comfortable chairs and the coffee is strong and *hot.* Colombian will be fine. Thanks!

M Club Letter

April 17, 2003
Ari Fleischer, Press Secretary, c/o The White House

Hi Ari,

What a great job you are doing! It is a good thing you are young because The M Club doesn't know how long a person could keep up the schedule you have been working. Americans sure appreciate the way you are keeping us informed by answering all those questions clearly and concisely. Keep up the good work, honey.

Ari, The M Club is writing to you today because of a comment you made recently. You said we should all "hope for the best but plan for the worst."

We want you to rethink that comment, Ari.

The M Club has done a *lot* of hoping and we have done a *lot* of planning. In case you didn't know or used to know but somehow forgot, The M Club is a group of millions of women between the ages of thirty-two and eighty-eight who have been in charge of everything from behind the scenes for many, many years. We were doing all this hoping and planning while you were still in grade school, Ari. We are good at hoping and planning.

Ari, we are pretty sure the statement you made is erroneous. We do *not* believe it is possible to "hope for the best and plan for the worst" at the same time. Please retract your comment the next time you go in front of that podium or do it by 5:00 p.m. EST today. (Don't call a special press conference for it or anything, but make sure you retract it the very next time you are up there, please.)

M Club members are sick and tired of other people getting the wrong message from reliable sources. You are a reliable source, Ari, and we are afraid a *lot* of people heard you say what you said.

Specifically, when M Club members "hope for the best," we put everything we've got into that hope. We put our hearts, our minds, our prayers, and our tears into hoping for the best. We have found it takes a *lot* of concentration to hope for the best. There is no way we "plan for the worst" while we are concentrating, because it takes away from the hoping. We have examples too!

Lisa Tarry, an M Club VIP member since 2003, hoped for the best for her two sons the whole time they were in high school. Hoping for the best is usually accompanied by action, so that whole family took steps to ensure the outcome of all that hoping. They all hoped those boys would get scholarships to the university, and they did! But Lisa *did not* ever go buy picks and shovels in an effort to "plan for the worst" so those boys could be ditchdiggers just in case that college thing didn't work out. *No!!*

We hope this example proves to you that a person cannot "hope for the best and plan for the worst" simultaneously. If one example doesn't convince you, Ari, The M Club has many more examples for your review.

So just retract your statement by 5:00 p.m. EST, or The M Club will have to come over there and tell you all our other examples of how it is impossible to "hope for the best but plan for the worst." If we must come over there, we will need a much bigger room than you use for those press conferences. We have forty million members and we *all* have an example of how hoping for the best is a concentrated effort that requires actions that don't include planning for the worst.

Looking forward to your retraction!

The M Club

P.S. In case we come over there, Gloria says to please make sure there are enough comfortable chairs and make sure the coffee is *hot*. Thanks.

M Club Letter

August 15, 2003
Post Office: Forward if Necessary
Ari Fleischer, Press Secretary, c/o The White House

Hi again, Ari,

Gee, The M Club didn't mean for you to *quit* over something as small as an erroneous comment. We miss you. Of course, we realize it is difficult to work that many hours for that many years and not get sick and tired of it. M Club members feel the exact same way sometimes.

Good luck and best wishes,

The M Club

M Club Mission

Today's M Club Mission is to find out how many *New York Times* editors read their own paper.

The M Club president was sipping her morning coffee and reading the newspaper. The only other mission she had planned for the day was planting some pansies and brushing The M Club mascot, Emma, a large, long-haired, black German shepherd who pretends to understand fake German words the Prez issues as scary-sounding commands when strangers knock on the door.

After reading a couple of pages of the newspaper, however, the Prez decided to make it her mission to find out exactly how many newspaper men and women read their own newspaper. The Prez figured not many editors were reading their own paper, because if they were they would see how easy it would be to solve some of these problems around here.

So she looked up the top guy at the *New York Times* and called him up:

"Hi, Arthur, this is the president of The M Club calling. I have made it my mission to find out exactly how many of your editors are reading your paper. Do you know?"

"I haven't the foggiest idea," Arthur said. "My mind is still foggy from reading reports in our paper that were totally made up." He added, "Great. Now I have another headache."

"Well, take a couple of Tylenol, Arthur, because you and I need to figure this out," the M Club president said. "You didn't recently quit drinking coffee, did you? You know that caffeine withdrawal will give people a headache sometimes. I read that in your paper."

"Okay, I've taken some Tylenol and refilled my coffee mug," Arthur responded.

"Okay, now open today's paper to page B7. Do you see the long article about the U.S. Department of Agriculture beginning to release the stockpile of 1.3 billion (one *point* three *billion*) *pounds* of powdered milk? See where it says this amount of powdered milk makes twenty-seven billion eight-ounce glasses of milk?"

"Wow! That is a *lot* of milk," Arthur said.

"Now, let's just turn the page to B8—just for a lark—and let's notice the *big* article there about the Ibero Summit, held in Bavaro, Dominican Republic," the Prez said. "It says twenty-one countries are meeting to figure out a way to 'confront poverty and debt,' and hopefully how to feed some of the people there they are so worried about."

"Yes, I see it," Arthur said. "We are on the same page."

"Art, The M Club wants this problem and this solution to get together. Right this minute. The problem and the solution are only one page apart. We think it is up to the newspaper men and women to read the damn paper. They already put the problem and the solution very nearly on top of each other. And you have a lot of reporters and telephones. The M Club wants your reporters to get on the damn phone and call the Department of Agriculture and set them up with the summit guys.

"Don't give us that excuse about not knowing the phone number," she continued. "Look it up! You have until 5:00 p.m. EST *today* to get that number and get on that phone or The M Club is *comin' over there*. If I have to look it up for you, you will be sorry. I am sick and tired of looking up numbers. Get busy. There are a *lot* of kids over there in need of a drink of milk."

"Yes, ma'am," Arthur said.

"I will give the Agriculture Department a call for you

and let them know you are sending some reporters over there," The M Club president offered, adding: "How's your headache doing, Arthur? You know I also read in your paper that headaches are sometimes caused by dehydration. Are you drinking enough water?"

"Yes. No. I don't know," Arthur said. "You know, you sound a *lot* like my wife!"

"Of course I do," the Prez said. "After all, your wife is *in* The M Club. Now get busy, Arthur. You've got some reporters to give this assignment to, and I've got another call to make. Don't forget to find out how many of your editors are actually reading their own paper. E-mail the answer to me by 6:00 p.m. EST, tonight."

"I'll do my best," Arthur said.

"That's all we expect, Arthur," the Prez said. "That's all we expect. Bye now."

The Prez poured another cup of coffee and looked up the head of the Department of Agriculture. Her name is Agriculture Secretary Ann M. Veneman and she has had the job since January 20, 2001.

"Hi, Ann, this is The M Club president calling," she said. "Please start getting that powdered milk packed up. Do it today. Do it by 5:00 p.m. EST, because there are a bunch of newspaper men and women coming over there to pick it up. They will deliver it to some people at a summit meeting in the Dominican Republic who are trying to figure out what to do about the poverty there.

"You know, you might have thought about this as a solution if you read the newspapers *or* if you had any imagination. The M Club has an imagination, so we figured it out for you," the Prez continued. "Don't waste time feeling bad because you did not think of this. Just get that milk packed up and ready to go. If The M Club has to *come over there,* we will. We have boxes, and we are good at packing and moving stuff. We have had to do it most of our lives."

"It's already packed up, ma'am," said Ann. "Jeanette? Is that you?"

"No, this is the president of The M Club," the Prez said.

"Sorry, you sound just like my secretary," she said. "I thought this was a joke."

"You think it's funny that your government agency has that much powdered milk sitting around when there are so many kids who are in need of some milk?" the Prez said, adding: "Say, if that milk is all ready to go, we have another request to make of you. While I've got you on the phone, would you mind telling me what kind of games you people are playing over there? Exactly what were you trying to accomplish by releasing billions of beetles in this country?"

"We were trying to find a natural way of killing aphids," she said, "but I wasn't agriculture secretary when that went down."

"Well, then it is up to you to get Daniel Robert Glickman on the phone and tell him that The M Club wants to know why he didn't think it through. Has he *no* imagination that might have given him a clue that releasing billions of those spotted beetles to eat some other agricultural threat might result in a whole new problem?" The Prez added, "You tell Dan that we are not buying that excuse of thinking of them as ladybugs. They are not ladybugs. We know this because ladybugs do not bite. Even if they were, we do not believe that old myth about ladybugs being good luck. A bug is a bug."

"The M Club wants Dan to know we are holding him personally responsible for ruining our vacuum cleaners. We had to vacuum those little suckers up at least once a day. He should know that if there is another swarm of those disgusting bugs on, in, or near our houses this fall, not only will he pay for new vacuums, he will also pay for house-cleaning, caulking, window-cleaning, and food that was touched by one of his bugs.

"Ann, maybe you could suggest to Dan that he give Hoover a call and make an arrangement, because we are sending him the bills for the first 2,075 new vacuums. We want them delivered *already assembled* to the homes of our M Club members. We also want a year's supply of new bags.

"Tell him he should get those vacuums ordered today by 6:00 p.m. EST. These women might *come over there* to your office. They are very polite, but some of them get hysterical over bugs, and I'm sure you have bugs over there that you experimented with to see which one would kill the aphids. Try to use your imagination to think how it would be to have a group of M Club members in your buggy office. It won't be pretty."

"What do you want me to do first—see to the powdered milk or give Dan a call?" Ann said.

"We don't care which you do first. You decide. Can we count on you to take care of both of these problems today?"

"You sure can," Ann said. "Makes sense to me!"

"Thanks, honey, it sure is good to have you over there to help take care of some of the things we see wrong around here," the Prez replied.

"No thanks are necessary, my dear," Ann said. "I am *in* The M Club."

M Club M-Mail
(formerly known as e-mail)

From:	TheMClub@aol.com
To:	pjennings@abcnews.com
Cc:	tbrokaw@nbcnews.com, drather@cbsnews.com, wblitzer@cnnnews.com, abrown@cnnnews.com, cgibson@abcnews.com
Date:	11/24/04 2:25:46 PM Eastern Standard Time
Subj:	What about the good news?

Hi, Peter, Tom, Dan, Wolf, Aaron, Charlie, etc.

You are doing it wrong. The M Club wants you to start choosing more positive stories to put on your nightly newscasts. Do it by tonight's show at 6:30 p.m. EST. It is up to you to figure out what time that will be in all the other time zones.

Here is the problem, gentlemen. You have been focusing on all the bad news for years and years. There is always a *lot* of bad news, but you only have thirty minutes for your shows, and you are using too much time on the bad things that are happening. You are doing it wrong.

Don't tell us that you indeed try to put in some good news reports. We watch your shows and only see one positive story per show. We do not want to hear that you report on the news as it happens and it seems to be all bad and that you can't help it.

The M Club knows there is a *lot* more good news that you are choosing not to include in your shows. We know you have lots of people behind the scenes for each individual network who choose the stories you will present to us. We want you to go tell them they need to choose *better* stories for you to read.

The effect of the way you have been doing it is tremendous. In case you haven't noticed, a *lot* of M Club members can't even watch your shows anymore. And as for the people who do keep watching all the bad stuff you tell them every single night, they are suffering from anxiety, depression, feelings of hopelessness, and other unhealthy symptoms. Some are eating too much, and your bad news is causing some to lose their appetites altogether. Of course, when people feel like this, they don't treat other people very well because they think nothing matters.

The M Club wants you *all* to get together and form a *new* television station to put all this bad news on. You can call it "Panic-Inducing News" or "Nightmare News with [anchor]" (insert your name). We don't care what you call your new news show, but if we don't see some immediate improvements by 6:30 p.m. EST today, *The M Club is comin' over there.*

We will be bringing all the good news stories about good things happening all around us every day to share with your audiences. We will pull up a couple of chairs next to you at your anchor desk. Then we will help you make everyone watching feel a *lot* better about the way things are going. At the end of the half-hour, you can tell everyone about the Panic-Inducing channel. People can still watch all that crap if they want to, but not on every single American national broadcasting time slot. After all, this is still America and people are still free to do what they want—within reason, of course.

Gentlemen, get busy sending all that copy over to the new channel. Do not waste time changing your set or your show format. Do not waste time going shopping for a new suit. In fact, wear the same suit you wore last night.

Then get busy gathering some *better* news to share. Don't tell us you can't find any. Look for it! We will bring enough to get you started.

See you tonight!

P.S. There is no need to promote The M Club as your new anchor team. We want it to be a surprise for all your viewers. And don't you dare come up with any clever wordplays like "Tonight's Broadcast by Real Broads" or "My Anchor Desk Is Sinking with the Weight of The M Club." Also, Debi says to make sure the coffee is *fresh* when we get there.

M Club Letter

March 18, 2004
Oprah Winfrey, c/o Harpo Studios

Hi, O, M here . . .

Have you fired that one attorney who drove into the McDonald's drive-thru the day you were working the window yet? We know it has been a while, but it has been a matter that we wanted to make sure was resolved, and we haven't heard it mentioned at all. We can't forget the way he talked to the person he thought was "just a McDonald's drive-thru worker."

To recap: You did a season premiere show about "regular people" and "good news" and went to a Chicago McDonald's restaurant to work a short shift at the drive-thru window. You joked with the people ordering food and got some really surprised looks on the faces of customers when they got to the window to pay and saw it was *you* working there. Then you bought their lunch for them. That was nice, O. No matter how much crap they bought the day you were there with your camera crew, you picked up the tab. You sure looked cute in that hat.

We were as surprised as you were when you said the guy ordering a meal sounded like your attorney! And in fact *it was your attorney!* But he didn't know it was *you* taking his order, and he was pretty rude. We know you thought he was rude too, because you even made a joke about it.

We were waiting for you to fire him as soon as he drove up to hand over his money. But you didn't. We think you should have said, "I'm sorry to embarrass you on national television, Bob, but I had no idea you were so rude, condescending, and impolite to "regular people," so *you are fired.* Also, I have been buying lunch for everybody who came through this drive-thru today, but because you were so nasty you will have to buy your own lunch."

We think you will agree that by your doing this a lot of people might have learned an impromptu lesson, Oprah, but you allowed the opportunity to slip by. After all, we are *all regular people.* We know you believe this too.

So did you fire him or not?

Please e-mail your answer to TheMClub@aol.com by 4:30 p.m. EST today. Thanks, honey. See you soon.

M Club President

M Club Letter

Fear Factor
Att: Executive Producers Matt Kunitz,
    David A. Hurwitz, and John de Mol, c/o NBC

Gentlemen,

Sorry, but your jobs are over as of 7:00 p.m. Pacific Time today. You have until then to clear out your offices and the sets you were using for that *Fear Factor* show. Make sure you get all those bugs out of there. When The M Club comes over there, they will not want to see *any* bugs. Of course, some of our forty million M Club members get hysterical about bugs, and we cannot be responsible for what might happen when we come over there.

Gentlemen, even though a *lot* of people are talking about your show, you are apparently not listening. So

The M Club is *comin' over there* to explain a few things to you. During our little chat, we will focus on key objections, including but not limited to:

- We have already taught everyone that fear is a God-given tool to tell each of us whether or not we should do anything. God gave us all that uncomfortable feeling in the pit of our stomachs, in addition to sweaty palms and a pounding heart, for a *reason*.

- You two have turned the whole concept around and somehow convinced people that it is *fun* to watch others do something against their common sense for *money*.

- We are producers too. We have produced the children who are getting the wrong message about *fear* because of your show. We are sick and tired of doing our work over again.

So, tonight, we want you to get in front of those television cameras *yourselves* (do *not* use that host) and tell everyone the show is over. Then tell them The M Club was right when we said, "No amount of money would be worth doing something you know in your heart is wrong, dangerous, stupid, or fear-inducing." Each of you must say those words three times. And you had better say it convincingly or else we will make you say it until you get it right. The M Club has members in transit who will be standing just off camera when you deliver this final speech.

Start practicing now, or use cue cards. We don't care how you learn your lines for tonight's finale, just learn them. Make sure you use the correct inflection and tone, because there are a *lot* of kids watching *Fear Factor*. In case you give any hint that you are not serious, we are prepared to strike fear in *you*, Matt, David, and John. You will recognize this feeling of fear by the uncomfortable feeling in the pit of your stomachs, your sweaty palms, and your pounding hearts. We suggest deep breathing when this fear strikes you all, but do what you want. And don't worry, in case ya'll faint while delivering *our* speech, don't forget we will be waiting in the wings to drag you off so you won't be embarrassed. See you tonight!

The M Club

CHAPTER 7

Money

The M Club's position on money is that the actual paper or coinage is, in itself, not as important as what good might be done with it. We all know money can't buy happiness or keep you warm on a cold night. It won't make you a better person either. Getting paid a lot of money for doing a job you hate doing is not worth it.

"Do something, anything, despicable for money and you will go straight to hell" might have been the eleventh commandment, which was unfortunately left off that stone tablet because it would have cost extra money to get it chiseled on. We were supposed to figure that out for ourselves, in our opinion.

By the time most regular women are *in* The M Club (Motto: We are *all* regular women, and we can prove it) they have gone through periods of having a little money or a lot of money. We realize at this point in our lives that, even when we didn't have much of the stuff, we always had *enough*. We know we are rich in the ways that really matter.

The M Club has actually been working on challenging a lot of old sayings. Frankly, we feel that a *lot* of old sayings are simply not true anymore. We don't care that they might have been true at some point, and we don't care where these sayings came from. One of our first M Club seminars dealt with the subject of money. It was a class titled "Money Is *Not* the Root of All Evil." The M Club sponsored the class and was forced to hold the seminar in a stadium because there are a *lot* of people who continued to believe in that saying.

Students learned where the root of all evil really is. It is not a root. It is not in the ground.

Students learned that there are many evils and that money is *one* root of evil but *not* the root of *all* evil.

Students learned that anytime, anywhere, anyone who thinks they are better than anyone else is the true root of evil. The class took a little longer than expected because the seminar was not over until everyone understood this new concept.

We filled in tracing-paper "trees" (much like a family tree), and then we traced evil back to its roots (much like a genealogy search). Students saw with their own eyes, right there in pencil on paper, that money is a *branch* of the tree. It is close to the roots because a lot of people who have a lot of money also think they are better than everyone else.

We had students bring their own pencils and paper. We asked them to bring lunch for themselves and to bring lunch for someone who might have forgotten their lunch. There was no place at the stadium to buy lunch because some of the founding members of The M Club *went over there* to the stadium before the class and gave all the vendors the day off. Besides, we are sick and tired of paying $10 for a hot dog and a soda.

M CLUB MEETiNG MiNUTES

Of course, a lot of clubs keep track of what happened at their meetings and even write it down. As you know, The M Club is sick and tired of keeping track. We have kept track of our children, our husbands, receipts for clothes we have already outgrown, and shoes for other people. However, we are happy to pass along discussion topics of other M Club meetings.

A small chapter of The M Club got together for coffee and cheesecake and watched Ellen DeGeneres perform in one of her fabulous HBO specials. At the end of this particular special, Ellen related a story about the waiting room she was in until it was her turn to talk to God.

After the show, Patsy Calmes (M Club member since 2003) said she thought there was also a waiting room near the Pearly Gates where new arrivals were interviewed about the subject of money.

"Welcome, Faye, so glad to see you here!" said the woman behind the desk, Ms. Dixon. "Can I get you anything—a cup of coffee, margarita, cookie, a pillow?"

"If you've got any decaf, I'll have some with just milk please," Faye said.

"We only serve the real thing here, Faye," Ms. Dixon said. "We are continually amused at the way everyone down there takes the good stuff out of everything and thinks it makes a difference!"

"Well, I don't want to be up all night," Faye said, confused.

"You don't need to worry about that anymore, honey," Ms. Dixon said. "Didn't you always say your idea of heaven was to be able to take a nap whenever you felt tired?"

Ms. Dixon opened her desk drawer and lifted out a steaming cup of strong coffee with real cream and passed it to Faye.

"Now, this first checkpoint interview is for one question and one question only," Ms. Dixon said. "The question is: Did you get the subtle irony of the whole 'money thing'?"

"I'm not sure what you mean," Faye said, sipping her coffee. "When I was younger, I always thought if money were anything else, I wouldn't have any of that either. However, I did learn that if I hadn't been short of money, I never would have come up with some resourceful ways of taking care of some things."

"Right! That was the first thing you were supposed to understand," Ms. Dixon said. "Anything else?"

"Well, I remember thinking I wouldn't ever be able to retire anyway so it was no use denying myself, my family, or my friends something they needed today because I had to 'save it for my golden years.' Besides, some of my friends died right after they retired and weren't able to use the money they had saved anyway. My motto was 'Carpe checkbooke,' meaning 'Seize the checkbook!'"

"Right again, Faye," Ms. Dixon said, refilling the coffee cup. "We saw the way you prioritized and gave money to your kids and friends instead of buying something for yourself. But what moved us the most was when you spent the car-payment money on a dress for your friend to wear to her son's funeral. You took her shopping and everything."

"That was nothing, really," Faye said, looking down.

"We're almost finished here, Faye," Ms. Dixon said. "Just one more question. If you could sum up your whole impression of the way it was down there about money, what would you say?"

Faye sipped her coffee and reflected for a moment.

"I guess I would say money wasn't very important, even though it seemed to be at times," Faye said. "When I look back, I always had *enough* and tried to make sure everyone I loved had enough. I never let it stand in my way of buying food or shoes or, later, a college education for my kids or that wheelchair for my neighbor's boy or, well, pretty much anything. If I didn't have it, I looked around until I found some money. Of course, I found money by working. I found out the government will lend money for college. Not all shoes cost $150. Sometimes I looked under the cushions of the sofa. Sometimes I looked in the phone book, like the time I called that wheelchair company and talked to that guy who had the wheelchair delivered to my neighbor's boy and never did send a bill. That company owner said he never thought about his own boy needing a wheelchair and that after I described Sean, my neighbor's boy, he said Sean sounded a *lot* like his own son. It's funny, the whole money thing down there seemed like a big game—there was plenty around and all I had to do was find it; it wasn't even hiding. It was always there when I needed it, anyway."

"Congratulations, Faye, you may step through that green door right over there," Ms. Dixon said, rising to give Faye a big hug. "That's the door for the people who knew they were rich no matter how much money they had. Everyone in there understood it wasn't the amount of money they had that mattered, it was what you were able to do with it that counted."

Faye went through the green door as Ms. Dixon called her next case.

"Jim Furgeson! How good to see you," Ms. Dixon exclaimed. "I was just talking about you with Faye! It says here you didn't ever send bills for 147 wheelchairs made by your company. Is that about right?"

"So I wasn't great at invoicing sometimes," Jim said. "Will a fault like that keep me out of here?"

"Not at all, Jim," Ms. Dixon replied. "Go right through the green door. And thanks."

M Club
Pitiful Excuse Aware

Our first M Club Pitiful Excuse Award goes to the Federal Bureau of Investigation. The M Club holds this government agency responsible for all the police departments all over the country who have not investigated crimes because they say they don't have enough money. We don't have time to go to each and every local police department, so, as usual, The M Club goes right to the top to try to fix some of the things we see wrong around here.

"What do you mean you don't have the money? Did you look under the sofa cushions?"

Our first case was brought to our attention when ABC News broke the story about rape evidence kits all over America sitting on dusty shelves in some back room instead of being used to catch rapists, because of the pitiful excuse of not having enough money to test them. These kits are collections of evidence that are supposed to be used in the apprehension and prosecution of criminals who rape women. The evidence is gathered at the hospital and should contain not only enough proof of the criminal act but also evidence of DNA belonging to the rapist that would prove the guilt of the creepy criminal. The officials said it cost $500 to test each kit.

When ABC News broke the story (thanks, ABC), the network paid to have twenty of these kits tested. Guess what? The DNA in almost half the evidence kits was put into a great big database with lots of criminal DNA already in it and *matches were found.* Then the police went and arrested the rapists.

The M Club definitely sees something wrong with this picture. So we came up with an idea to fix this problem. Here are the letters we sent, and we will let you know as soon as we hear something:

M Club Letter

March 20, 2004
U.S. Department of Transportation
Att: Norman Y. Mineta

Hi Norm,

A few changes are needed in your department before another summer of construction on American highways is underway.

The M Club wants you to go state by state and make sure the scheduled roadwork for the upcoming season is really needed. Also, take a look at the numbers of employees you have on all these jobs.

This is your responsibility, Norman. We are sick and tired of states bragging about getting huge portions of tax money for their roads. We are also sick and tired of seeing too many men standing around in orange safety vests. If they are standing around, there is not enough work for them on the site.

We want you to send the extra men, the ones who were standing around, over to the FBI office. We want you to give these thousands of men a standardized test. If they pass the test and if they are wearing pants that do not slip way below their hips, we want them working for the FBI from now on. You will have to keep paying them, because you have a lot of road money.

Tell them their new job is to test the rape evidence kits that have piled up all over America. Are you aware that standard procedure is to collect DNA evidence after a woman is raped and that, while the victim thinks the police are working to catch the degenerate, the authorities actually aren't doing *anything* with the evidence because they whine about not having the five hundred bucks it costs to test the evidence? Did you know ABC News paid to have twenty evidence kits tested last summer and more than half of those were put into the FBI database and *matches were found and the criminals were finally jailed?*

The M Club is sure the highway men can do this testing, and you can pay for it, Norman. It should be a simple test. Then they can enter the data into the huge database that already has lots of criminal DNA statistics in it. We think they will find a lot of matches. Tell them to turn the matches over to the FBI so these criminals can be put in jail finally. These men will be relocating from every state. It is up to you to tell them to *bring* the dusty rape evidence kits from their state *with* them.

The men who find the most matches will get the extra reward of getting to tell the victims, "We got that despicable creep, and he will never hurt you or any other woman again." Winners will also get to tell their own little girls that America is a *lot* safer now because their daddies are working hard on catching these degenerates. It will be a good feeling for these dads.

We want to know how many extra men you will be sending by Friday at 5:00 p.m. EST. Get busy.

Anne Ewing
M Club Coordinator

M Club Letter

March 20, 2004
Federal Bureau of Investigation
Att: Director Robert Mueller, III

Director Mueller:

Please clear out some of that old crap over there, because the U.S. Department of Transportation is sending over a bunch of new employees for you. They will be testing the rape evidence kits that have piled up all over the country.

Don't panic, Mueller. They are bringing the kits. You don't have to collect them.

Your job right now is to find a *better* way to test the DNA in these kits so the highwaymen can match it to your database. You must not have looked very hard if the best price you could find to test a single kit was $500. Look again. Look for a cheaper price.

The M Club is good at finding discount prices on a million products and services. But we are busy taking care of a *lot* of other things around here, so we think you should do it. Tip: Check over there at the Patent and Trademark Office. *Walk* over there, Bob. It is right down the street from your office. There are probably new and better ways to test those rape kits. They are probably cheaper too. It is up to you to find out.

Meredith Bakersfield
M Club member since 2003

 # M Club Letter

January 23, 2004
The Hanes Corporation
Att: C. Steven McMillan, Chairman,
      President, and CEO

Mr. McMillan,

You are spending too much money on underwear commercials. The only choices we have are your company, the underwear with the fruity guys, and a few others. Everybody needs underwear, and they buy it when they need it. You will not sell any more underwear than you are now because of your commercials.

The M Club wants you to stop spending all that money advertising underwear. We are sick and tired of seeing people dance in their jockey shorts. It is okay with us if people want to dance in their jockey shorts, but we do not want to see it anymore.

We want you to use the money you will save on advertising to send new underwear to hospitals to *give* to patients. We don't think grown adults should have to wear a gown with a big slit up the back with no underwear on. It is embarrassing.

With other money you will save after you stop paying to have nearly naked people dancing on television, we want you to assign some designers to come up with better hospital attire. Hospital gowns have been the same for too long. We are counting on you to fix this problem because you already have all that cotton cloth in pretty colors.

Thanks, Steven. Maybe you would have thought of this yourself if you had any concern for other people. But it never hurts to point out the obvious, in our opinion, as long as it is done in a polite way.

Looking forward to your new line by March!

Sissy MacDonald
M Club member since 2003

P.S. We are sure you can do this, especially because, according to you Web site, "Hanes responded to a lack of laundering facilities" and apparently "airlifted underwear to the international press in the small village of Lillehammer for the 1994 Winter Olympic Games in Norway!"

M Club Mandate

Today is the deadline for the end of using money as any means of reward for anything. If this is your first notice, that is too bad. The M Club knows some Americans are too busy spreading around gossip about other people, so that will teach you to start talking about some real news that *is* your business.

Americans are hereby notified that, henceforth, money will not be used as a reward anymore, ever again, and that is final. We mean: pennies, nickels, dimes, quarters, half-dollars, silver dollars, as well as paper money, including any and all denominations.

Is this specific enough for you? We mean *any kind of money.*

The stuff is responsible for too much crap that we see wrong around here, including but not limited to: kids going for the grade instead of learning, anyone perform-ing a kind act for another person for money instead of helping them out because they are a *person*, kids getting paid to do chores instead of doing them to help their fam-ilies, and many other infractions. You get the idea.

We are not talking about the reward of getting money for your work, even though we think work should be its own reward. We have to pay the electric bill too. But if the money you get from your job is not even rewarding, and you hate the job too, *quit*. Get a newspaper and find another job. Someone else would love to have your job. Life is too short to not have any rewards.

It's a new year, folks. We're starting off fresh. No more money as a reward for anything. I am the attorney for The M Club, and they will know if you keep it up. The M Club is enormous now, and you know how people gossip. One of them is sure to hear about it.

Think of other rewards you will get for doing things. Here are a couple to get you started: a nice, warm feeling; a tight embrace; the thanks of a stranger; a smile from a child; a smile from God—you get the idea.

Camille Doyle

M Club attorney

M Club Seminar

October 19, 2004

Dayton, OH—The M Club will teach a seminar at the University of Dayton on Tuesday, October 19, 2004. There is no registration, because we are sick and tired of lists. The class is free because we think education has gotten way too expensive. Hope you can join us!

"BILLS, BILLS, BILLS."

This is not a class for men named Bill, although they are certainly welcome to join us. This class will teach students to stop thinking so much about the bills they owe and start thinking about other things they owe.

Topics covered include:

- Do I owe a favor?
- Do I owe a kind word to a stranger?
- Do I owe respect to people who don't scare me?
- Do I owe myself a day off?
- Do I owe anyone an apology?
- Do I owe anyone long overdue thanks?
- If you write the word "owe" a lot, doesn't it start to look misspelled?

If you answered no to any of the above topics, you need this class. If you answered yes to the above topics and haven't paid up with the favor, respect, kind word, apology, day off, or thanks, you also need this class. Meet by the pond. You owe it to yourself. See you there.

A MESSAGE FROM THE PRESIDENT

September 28, 2004

Hello, M Club Members,

Remember the public announcement when the founding members got up at 2:00 a.m. EST on July 3, 2002, so we could see the Delta II launch at Kennedy Space Center from the beach?

Remember we were questioning why only twenty-five people had gotten up to watch it?

Well, now I know why.

In the September 2 edition of *Space News* there is a great big article titled "Discussions Begin on Possible Contour Replacement." It caught my eye when one of the men in my house left the paper on the bathroom floor.

Anyway, I was very disheartened when I read that they need to replace the Contour because the one I saw get launched *is lost*. It might even be broken, because they can see three pieces instead of one piece where the Contour is supposed to be up there in space.

As you may remember, but probably not, the Contour was a Comet Nucleus Tour (CONTOUR) spacecraft launched with the help of the Delta II rocket. The Contour was supposed to go study some insides (nuclei) of some comets.

It cost $159 *million* to make it, not including the money it cost to get it up in space. I don't know how much that was, but I bet it was a *lot*.

"So obviously we're not very optimistic about the chances of ever recovering Contour again. However, we haven't given up totally. There's an obligation to make sure that the spacecraft is indeed lost," said Robert Farquhar, Contour Mission Director.

Now I know why there were only twenty-five people on the beach. They thought like I used to think. I used to think it was an incredible feat of human engineering, intelligence, a little magic thrown in, a lot of work by a lot of talented people, and a real statement concerning the way we humans can dream of something, anything, and make a dream come true.

I don't think that anymore. Those guys spent all that money and they lost it. It is gone.

I am still glad I saw my first-ever launch. But when somebody loses something worth that much, The M Club feels compelled to write a letter to the one in charge. If this letter doesn't work, we'll have to *go over there* to explain it better. We'll let you know how we make out. Meanwhile, if any M Club members have time to *go over there* with us, we could meet by the pond.

Best,

M Club President

M Club Letter

September 28, 2002
Robert Farquhar
Contour Mission Director
NASA / Kennedy Space Center

Director Farquhar:

The M Club is glad you are not giving up hope about finding your lost Contour spacecraft. We believe in hope. We hope for the best in many situations. We hope you find the Contour.

But we read that you want to replace the Contour (Reference: *Space News*, September 2, 2002, page 21).

We want you to stop talking about replacing it. You already lost one, and we don't think you should take a chance on losing another one. Besides, the one you lost cost $159 million, and with inflation it would cost a *lot* more to replace it. Did you have replacement insurance on it?

Do you know what your mother would think, Robbie? She would think you should not get another Contour because you couldn't keep track of the one you had. Just like that expensive baseball mitt she got you when you begged, pleaded, and cried at the store. She got you that mitt, and then what did you do? You lost it. She would not buy you another one because you couldn't keep track of your belongings. You should have put your name on your mitt.

The M Club does not want to hear any begging, pleading, or crying this time, Robbie. You may *not* have another $159 million for another Contour, because you still cannot keep track of your belongings. It is not your fault. We are sick and tired of keeping track of a lot of things too. We have kept track of our children, our husbands, days of the week, and shoes for other people. We know keeping track is hard. Did you put your name on the Contour?

We want you to tell those other guys at the next meeting about replacing the Contour that you have changed your mind. Tell them, "It might turn up sometime, but right now we can't spend another $159 million." Then say, "Let's give the Department of Defense the money we would have spent on another Contour because they can use that money today."

You tell those fellows, or The M Club will come over there, Robbie. We can find you because we are good at finding things. We could probably find your lost Contour, but we think when you lose something in a place as big as space, it might be too hard. We also want you to make those guys *keep looking*. Don't tell us you can't find it until you look for a longer time. Look again.

Thanks for taking care of this, Robbie. Hope you find it!

M Club President

M Club M-Mail

From:	TheMClub@aol.com	⬆⬇
To:	All major television network CEOs	
Date:	February 11, 2004	
Subj:	Super Bowl commercial time slots	

Gentlemen:

You have a good eleven months to change the way you are all selling advertising time slots for ridiculous sums of money. The M Club wants you to start working on this problem by 8:00 a.m. EST on Tuesday, February 24, 2004, so you will be ready for next year.

In case you didn't know, The M Club is a group of forty million women who are sick and tired of hearing about the millions of dollars you are collecting to air new commercials during the Super Bowl time slots. Most of us don't even *watch* the game because we have a *lot* of other things to do. However, we know you are charging way too much money for certain companies to advertise on one night in January every year.

Stop it. Stop now or The M Club is *comin' over there.* We will be coming from a variety of locations all around this great country. We will be bringing our local newspapers with any number of articles we have circled in *red* that tell about a *lot* of problems around here. Many of these articles inform us about big problems or small problems. The thing all these articles have in common, apparently, is that a lack of money is causing many people a problem.

And what do you do *every January?* You charge unheard-of prices to let companies play a one-minute commercial during a game? What in the *hell* have you been doing with all that money anyway? We can't remember what game number you are on, is it XXII or XXXIV? Whatever number game it is, this thing has gone on for too long.

The M Club wants a preliminary idea of how you will be solving this problem by 9:00 p.m. EST on Monday. Send the preliminary ideas to TheMClub@aol.com, please. Make sure you have at least ten good suggestions for what you would do with that money. It is up to you to collect the money from those companies, and we want a written report of any networks that balk at this new idea.

Let's face it, gentlemen, if they can pay all that money for a sixty-second commercial, they can save their commercials and *give* the money to you anyway. You are already set up to collect those billions, so it is up to you to redistribute it *better.*

Maybe you could tell those companies that M Club members are the ones who buy stuff (mostly) and that we aren't even watching those expensive commercials, so the whole thing is a great big waste of time. We don't care what you tell them, just make sure they understand that if this thing isn't fixed by next January there might not *be* a game. The M Club will go over there and collect all those footballs, and nobody will be able to play the damn game. We will be calling our plan "The M Club Has Balls But You Don't." Of course, the fans will blame you.

Thanks for taking care of this! See you soon!

The M Club

M Club Memo

To: Collection Agencies in America
From: The M Club

Your jobs are over, so pack up all your crap and leave your offices by noon tomorrow (12:00 p.m. EST).

It is not your fault that your jobs are terminated. It is the economy. You see, the only threats you have to make to us to get us to pay that old bill are not valid anymore. When you threaten to ruin our credit ratings, we laugh out loud. Everyone knows you can't follow through on your threat, especially because we keep getting *already approved* credit cards in the mail. Every day. We even get them for our children, whom we advise not to sign up for that seemingly free $5,000 until they are at least twelve.

Also, you know and we know that there is a law protecting us from telephone harassment. All we have to do is say, "Don't call me anymore." Then, if you call again, you are harassing us. It might be called the harassing law. Anyway, you get in big trouble for harassment these days.

So you can't call us and your written threats are no good. Your jobs are finished. You can do no more.

Besides, we have never taken you seriously. Some of us got letters from collection agencies the day before we had to pick out clothes for our children to be buried in. Some of us got those letters when we came home from a sixty-two-hour vigil at a loved one's hospital bed. Most of us, however, are pretty damn busy taking care of husbands, children, grandchildren, pets, and others. We don't even have time to read your mean letters.

You all will find better jobs soon. We have spoken with you, and you are very nice people. We like you. We think you probably didn't like that job anyway.

Quit or take this notice seriously. It's up to you, but your job is over now.

Thanks, and have a nice day.

M Club Mandate

The M Club has polled our *forty million members* and wanted to let you Americans know that from now on, forevermore, and this is final, we will not be using the phrase "give-and-take" anymore.

The M Club has changed the phrase to "give-and-give."

Sure, life is full of give-and-take situations. However, The M Club noticed there was a *lot* more taking going on than giving. As you know, The M Club's forty million members are sick and tired of keeping track: we have kept track of our children, our husbands, our silverware, and shoes for other people. Even though we have not kept track of the amount of giving-and-taking, it sure seems to us that there needs to be more giving.

The new phrase "give-and-give" will take effect at 6:00 p.m. EST today. Please make a note. Write it on your calendar or write it on your hand. We don't care where you write it down. Just be sure to start giving and giving instead of giving and taking.

Guess what? There will be a *lot* of improvements around here because of that domino effect thing, where giving something will cause the *givee* to become the *giver* in one great big giving cycle. This could be big, folks. This is not exactly like that "random acts of kindness" fad that fizzled out pretty quickly. This should last a *lot* longer, because The M Club wants this giving to be not random (*specific* is what we are going for here).

As far as we can tell, those random acts of kindness fizzled out because there were a lot of ungrateful people who didn't deserve an act of kindness and knew they didn't deserve it. They probably felt they had no business passing it on because they think the world owes them already. We will not be able to change their minds about this.

What we will be able to do, however, is to reward *deserving* givers with other giving. For example, Jackie Roth, M Club member since '03, bought an extra basket of pansies when she bought her own spring flowers, and presented it to Cathy Johnson, the Wal-Mart assistant manager, the very next time she shopped at the store. Of course, Cathy was surprised. "I was just doing my job," she said. "I didn't expect any thanks."

But Cathy doesn't get paid enough in money to go *above and beyond* like she did. Cathy was able to put herself in Nancy's place, a trait most M Club members share. She gave of herself and she should be rewarded. As Jackie said, "It cost $3.97 for an extra basket of pansies. I have *that* much under the cushions of my couch. *So what!*"

The M Club knows that a *lot* of our members are already doing this. We give other members our thanks, and then we give something else. We send some flowers. Sometimes we take lunch over to her at work. We give her some time and ask about her daughter. We give her some hope about the way things are improving around here by showing her we appreciate what she did. We give friendship. We give her boss a call and tell him what a great employee he has working for him. We give whatever we can think of, and we are *not* surprised at the way the givee becomes the giver in one great big giving cycle.

M Club Celebrity Interview

*Today's celebrity is Murline Steward, a
forty-seven-year-old woman from Tupelo, Mississippi.
Murline is a celebrity because she got a stuffy old
bank to see things in an unstuffy new way.*

M CLUB PRESIDENT: Thank you for speaking with us today, Murline, on this important subject of money!

MURLINE: Well, I always make time to give others a sense of what might be possible in a lot of different situations. I have been doing that for years and years. Finally my experience with creditors has paid off.

M CLUB PRESIDENT: So it seems. Please tell us your story in your own words.

MURLINE: Well, it all started when I went into my neighborhood bank and was assaulted with signs all over the place. There were signs hanging from the ceiling. There were signs on every door. There were signs next to all the tellers. The signs advertised a new slogan for the bank. They all said "Yes." The signs implied that if you needed to borrow any money, this bank was going to say "Yes." They even told people calling them, "Hello, ask me about money—we say Yes!" when they answered the phone.

M CLUB PRESIDENT: Wow! Sounds like you have a great bank.

MURLINE: Well, that's what I thought. I mean, I owe them seven times what my house is worth if I pay off the mortgage in thirty years; I pay them loan-shark prices for the one credit card they were only too happy to give me; and I pay an extra $32 every time my credit-card payment is six minutes late. I feel sure I am financing *someone's* Bahamas vacation! Anyway, my banker is like a friend. We see each other around town and always say hello. So I was surprised when I went in there to borrow a little bit of money for an emergency and she said "No."

"But what about all of your "Yes" signs you have all over this place?" I asked her. "And don't you think it would be more fair to hang a few "No" signs up too, instead of getting my hopes up like that? Did you consider using a roulette wheel as a background for your slogans? I mean, if you are only taking a chance on getting a "Yes," shouldn't we *know* it is going to be a gamble, not a sure thing?"

M CLUB PRESIDENT: Instead of a roulette wheel, what about a crapshoot table, like in casinos, for a logo?

MURLINE: Speaking of crap, the reason I was turned down for the home-equity loan was because of a few late payments in the last two months, the banker said. Also, I had arranged for a deferment on my car, which I thought made good sense. This also showed up on my credit report.

M CLUB PRESIDENT: You mean when you were up-front and honest about having temporary trouble, and did the right thing, and were up-front and honest about a problem, you were penalized for it?

MURLINE: Apparently. Do you see why M Club members get so frustrated?

M CLUB PRESIDENT: What did you do?

MURLINE: I wrote my own credit report to show the bank. I thought they should look at all the times I have not been six minutes late. I thought they should consider if it was their own daughter who suffered an automobile accident and was forced to come home after living on her own for three years. I asked if they too wouldn't have bought a bed for her so they could take care of her at home for a few months. I asked if they didn't think a bed for their own daughter was more important than a car payment. I didn't want to use my personal problem as an excuse because I am sick and tired of excuses. However, that underwriter needed to know that I am a person, that my daughter is a person, and that a car is not as important as a person! Besides, I can catch up on the car payments, thanks to the deferment.

M CLUB PRESIDENT: How did it work out for you?

MURLINE: Well, I was approved, finally. But I don't know if I will take the loan or not. I still need to decide. At least I might have helped the next M Club member who comes in and expects a "Yes" from that awful advertising. I know they have a *lot* of customers, but we aren't just a number. We are people who need help sometimes. We kept our promise to pay a *lot* of times before, and we are a good risk because we keep our promises. Here is the graph I used to get the bank to look at all the times I paid on time instead of the few times I had a little trouble. I also use this graph as a handy template for hanging my outdoor Christmas lights.

Murline's Version of Her Credit Report

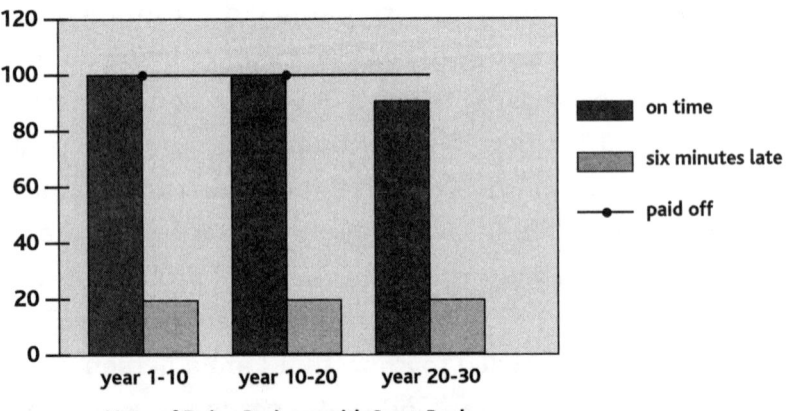

M CLUB PRESIDENT: Thank you for sharing your story today, Murline. We can all learn a lesson from the way you showed other people you are a person and not a number, and that you are able to keep a promise when you make one.

MURLINE: You're welcome, Prez. But speaking of promises,

is there anything The M Club can do about all the promises made around here that are not kept?

M CLUB PRESIDENT: We can offer to teach an M Club seminar about promises again, the way M Club members have taught about promises and other important things for years and years. And years.

CHAPTER 8

Advice and Etiquette

M Club members have discovered that giving advice seems to be a lot of wasted breath, especially when we were not asked for the advice. We waste money, time, paper, tears, and a *lot* of other things, but we hardly ever waste breath.

The other reason we rarely give advice is that we find people must learn their own lessons and that they do what they feel is correct at the time. We are able to be a sounding board for problems; however, we shy away from telling people exactly what they should do. They will do what they want to do despite our advice. Our way of looking at advice-giving prevents us from having to say "I told you so," which we feel is not helpful to anyone. We are working on a line of greeting cards that do say "I told you so," but writing it and saying it are two different things, of course.

In our everyday dealings with people, members of The M Club are often asked advice on etiquette. "What should I do?" a woman will ask a friend. "What was I supposed to say?" a child will ask a parent. "And by the way, where are my shoes?" that same child will ask.

It may come as a surprise to M Club members that the word "etiquette" and the word "ethics" come from different languages and have different meanings. The former is a French word meaning "a thing attached, a label." The definition of "etiquette" is "conventional forms of ceremony or decorum." Meanwhile, that Webster fellow says the word "ethic" (ethical) is from the Greek word for "custom" or "habit" and is defined as "relating to morals." So we can see that, by definition and origin, the two words seem to have little in common. However, the words are linked in some way, not only in the minds of M Club members but also by that Webster fellow—this time in his thesaurus. It is a roundabout way, but the words are connected like this:

Etiquette ⟶ conduct ⟶ manners ⟶ social graces
⟶ (see behavior) ⟶ behavior ⟶ deportment
⟶ conduct ⟶ manners ⟶ actions ⟶ morals
⟶ social graces ⟶ ethics

We can see that even though "etiquette" and "ethics" started out differently, they came together as meaning almost the same, which is the leading reason that a recent survey of our *forty million* M Club members confirmed that most people already know what they should do; that it is not so difficult to do the right thing; and that reading the dictionary is always a good way to come up with something to think about.

When asked advice or questions about etiquette, The M Club answers politely and without making the questioner feel idiotic. M Club members are able to see right from wrong very clearly and can ignore immaterial, extraneous information in any type of question. We have had a *lot* of practice with this and have answered questions from children as young as fifteen months of age. Repeatedly. Over and over. The same question.

Our answers are given with an economy of words, in an even tone. Whether we use a clenched jaw and/or grit our teeth is entirely dependent on the question. Many questions may be answered with a question to the person asking advice. "What would your mother think?" is a favorite of ours. We like to give people a chance to figure things out themselves, and we think they already know many answers themselves. You see, we taught these people right from wrong years ago. Sometimes they need a reminder, that's all.

M Club Q & A

Q: Is there any way to tell by looking at a person if they have any compassion?

> Julianne Bradfield
> Butte, Montana

A: Unlikely. You might try looking into their eyes. Sometimes you can see their heart, but this is not reliable. Looking at a person's actions is the method M Club members use. Good luck.

A LiTTLE M CLUB ADViCE
(just a little)

Just a reminder that if any Club members are under the impression that God is a pitcher for a baseball team, we would like you to think about that a little more.

This matter came to our attention when an M Club member said recently, "Every time things are looking up and everything is going fine in my life, God throws me a curveball and I almost fall apart."

Her voice was cracking when she said it. Then she cried.

The M Club does not believe God throws curveballs. He doesn't throw anything. He is busy taking care of a *lot* of other things around here, and he doesn't have time to throw curveballs.

Sure, God gave lots of those pitchers the talent for pitching. We have seen pitchers throw a ball up to ninety-nine miles an hour, and they even threw it right where they wanted it to go. Those guys pitch fastballs, slow balls, curveballs, changeups, and other balls (you get the idea).

Okay, okay, God might play baseball sometimes, but we don't think he *aims* the ball at anyone in particular. He said we were all special; he said he is there for *all* of us. He was not playing games when he said that.

So, just as a reminder, please don't say God has thrown us a curveball when something goes wrong. Usually, some *person* threw that curveball that is upsetting you. Our advice is to do what the batters at the big-league games do when a pitcher is pitching to them:

- Stand firm.
- Get ready.
- Keep your eye on it.
- Swing like hell.

Even if it was a curveball, we can all face it at home plate. When the game is over, go *home*. Things may look better tomorrow.

M Club Q & A

Q: Why did my friend break a promise she made to me?

> Allysa Behm
> Miami, Florida

A: We don't know. Maybe she needs to go to the seminar sponsored by The M Club titled "How to Keep a Promise." There is one in your area soon. Good luck.

M Club Seminar
June 30, 2004

Florida State University—The M Club will sponsor a summer session at Florida State. The classes are free. There is no registration.

PROMISES, PROMISES

Students will discover new and exciting facts about promises. Students will learn what a promise is, when to make a promise, when not to make a promise, and how to keep a promise.

The M Club has been aware for some time that many Americans are getting this wrong. Participants must promise to take notes so that students will be able to refer to something whenever they even think about making a promise.

This class has been requested by the many other Americans who are sick and tired of promises being made to them and not kept. We are talking about *any* kind of promise. Some of the promises covered in this class include:

"I promise I won't tell."

"I promise I will do that."

"I promise I will never do that again."

"I promise you the moon and the stars."

Etc. (you get the idea).

Then we will cover how to keep a promise. Students will learn not to make a promise they can't or won't keep, or have no intention of keeping. We have ideas on where to keep promises, including:

In your heart

In your head

In your top dresser drawer next to the baby teeth

In case students learn quickly because they used to know about promises but somehow forgot, The M Club promises to take everybody to the beach. Bring bathing suits. Debi says to also bring SPF 48 sunblock.

M Club Seminar
May 1, 2004

Dateline America—A new class will be taught by The M Club at our new university, IMU. (School mottos: "I am the same as you"; "I could be you"; "We are all in this together"; "IMU: The university with a *lot* of mottos"; and "If you think you are better than us, this school is not for you") There is no registration for M Club classes because we are sick and tired of keeping track of names on lists. We have kept track of our children, our husbands, baby teeth, and shoes for other people. We are also sick and tired of lists. M Club classes are free. We are sick and tired of education being so expensive.

This class has been requested by the many M Club members who have an apology coming to them. We think people who need to apologize might have forgotten how, or might not know how, and that could be the reason for withholding the apology. The M Club will teach "How to Make an Apology" at 1:00 p.m. EST on May 15, 2004. Meet by the pond at IMU.

Students will learn how easy it is to apologize to anyone, anywhere, anytime with the simple words "I'm sorry." Students will learn that there is no expiration date on apologies; an apology is welcome immediately following a cruel comment or action, or days, weeks, months, or years after the infraction has occurred. M Club members will give examples of how two words can save a relationship.

Insincere apologies will be examined. We will debate the effectiveness of an apology that is heartfelt, one that is not heartfelt but could be at a later date, and one that has been made repeatedly for the same infraction. We will examine these specific apologies:

> "I'm sorry to tell you this, but you seem to be an idiot." (Is this really an apology?)
>
> "I'm sorry. I didn't do that for you, and I really have no intention of doing it in the near future." (Is this a real apology?)
>
> "I'm sorry," followed by the very same infraction over and over again. (How much is this apology worth?)
>
> Etc. (you get the idea)

Students will learn that making an apology is not the same as changing one's position on a matter. It is made because another person's feeling are hurt.

Then students will enjoy a quick refresher course on "How to Accept an Apology." The M Club will show how accepting an apology is just as difficult as making an apology sometimes. We will also cover which "inconveniences" may and may not be covered by an apology. One example we will examine is the slew of printed apology advertisements in every single Sunday newspaper that apologize for the company's advertisement that ran the very same day and that say the price printed was wrong.

Meet by the pond at 1:00 p.m. EST sharp. The M Club will not accept excuses for tardiness. We will, however, accept an apology in case a student is late. See you there!

M Club Mandate

America is hereby informed that too much time is being spent making decisions on anything from what excuse to use to what to do if you are asked a favor.

It does not take much time to decide on doing the right thing, folks.

From now on, The M Club has set a deadline for *any* type of decision. Americans will have thirty seconds from the time anyone says "Make up your mind."

Think of it as a game. Everyone knows Americans like to play games.

The M Club wants you to know that we have made decisions in *split* seconds, and we feel thirty seconds is long enough to decide what the right thing to do is. It is easy because you all already know what the right thing is. Concentrate on the words "What would your mother think?" It will be close enough. M Club members all over the country will be timing your thirty seconds. We can tell how long thirty seconds is without a stopwatch because we have had to time *contractions*.

Let the games begin!

Public Announcement

To: All book reviewers at all
newspapers and magazines

The M Club has had enough, folks. All of you book reviewers with nothing but mean things to say are fired. Clean out your desks by 5:00 p.m. EST today. If you are working from home on a computer, an M Club member will be there shortly to pick it up. We have boxes.

Folks, don't you remember what your mother told you? Yes, you can. You can even hear her voice. She said, "If you can't say something nice about someone, don't say anything at all."

Your reviews will not be needed anymore, ever again, and that is final. That author worked hard to write that book. Books are a lot harder to write than short reviews like yours, you know. The publishers thought it was good work or they would not have published it. It is up to shoppers to decide if they want to buy it or not.

It is not up to you to tell us whether or not to buy it.

You are fired.

Don't give us that excuse about wanting to warn people not to waste their money. That is no excuse. We have all wasted a *lot* of money. We have wasted money on shoes that felt perfectly comfortable at the store that turned out to be awful. We have wasted money buying the exact duplicate of an expensive coat our kids told us they lost, only to have the lost coat turn up again the day we bought the new one. We don't care about wasting money.

We do care about wasting breath, though. And you book reviewers have wasted quite enough breath.

You will have to find another job now. You should all consider something other than the writing field. If you do stay in writing, we want you to write something nice for a change.

The M Club

M Club Seminar
November 1, 2004

Chicago, IL—Many new and unconventional classes will be offered at Northwestern this spring semester. The university is not in any way affiliated with these classes, but they will be held on campus in serene locations outdoors. The university tried to make us pay to teach there and were unreasonable about the amount of money they demanded for the use of regular classrooms. So the classes will be held outdoors. The classes are free. The topics are varied. Here are the classes that are scheduled. Many others will be added before spring.

Session 1:
EXCUSES, EXCUSES

Lively discussions will highlight the many excuses people use to dodge many responsibilities. Participants must bring a list or recite the whoppers they have heard over the years. There are no awards for the best excuse; excuses will not be judged for their effectiveness. All excuses for dodging responsibility will be treated the same—The M Club will have them stricken from the English language for good.

Students will learn how to recognize an excuse when they hear one. Students will also learn how to deal with anyone, anytime, anywhere who offers an excuse for despicable behavior.

"That Is No Excuse" bumper stickers, pens, and baseball caps will be given to the first one thousand students taking the class. There is no registration. Just show up at the big tree near the pond at Northwestern on April 1, 2005. See you there.

Session 2:
GLARINGLY SIMPLE

This class will teach *The M Club Glare* to students having a hard time getting their messages across.

There is not a lot of talk in this class. Students can't talk and learn how to glare convincingly at the same time. Be prepared to work in this class, however, because it takes practice to get a message across with a glare.

Participants who are worried about what "The Glare" will do to the lines on their foreheads or lines around their eyes will be sent downtown to shop. This class is not for you.

There is no registration. Just show up at the pond at Northwestern on the side *across* from the big tree. Don't be afraid to approach the group already there. They are just practicing their glares. Hope you can join us.

M Club Mandate

The rules have changed concerning lines. The M Club has been concerned over lines for years. No, not lines on our faces. We mean lines to get in to anyplace.

From now on, the first one in line for anything must step aside politely. Just because you were there first doesn't mean anything anymore.

The people who should go to the front of any line are the ones who had the most difficult time getting to the line. For instance, a young mother with three or more toddlers goes to the front automatically. Anyone who could not start the car and cried because she was afraid she would be late gets to go next. Anyone experiencing any type of mishap on the way to said line will go next. You get the idea.

We do not want to hear that just because you are organized, have no children, have a good car, have time, or have the wherewithal to get someplace on time, you should be first in line. We want you to have patience with those who came after you, because most times it is not their fault they arrived disheveled, out of breath, and with tearstained cheeks. Cut them some slack and let them cut in line.

The point here is: Cutting in line is a good thing. There will be no more mean comments or fighting about lines. In fact, The M Club wants the whole line to applaud for both the cutter and the cuttee. We all will get through the line eventually, so The M Club says, "What's the big deal?"

It might just get you a better position in that line at the Pearly Gates, you know. Thanks.

M Club Seminar
June 15, 2004

Boston, MA—Many new classes will be offered during summer semester at Harvard next month. The classes are not in any way affiliated with the university. The M Club doesn't care who gets credit for the new classes, however, because they have been needed for a *long* time.

The classes are free.

BUT, BUT, BUT

This class is designed to make people quit using the word "but." The M Club has stricken it from the English language, in case you haven't heard. Without this word, conversations in America will begin to take on a more polite tone. This is the goal of the class.

Session 1 (July 1–15) will concentrate on deleting the following phrases from our language:

> "It's none of my business, *but . . .*"
> "I don't mean to offend, *but . . .*"
> "I didn't mean to hurt your feelings, *but . . .*"
> "You didn't ask me, *but . . .*"

We are looking for a *nonmenopausal man* to teach this class. Sara Martin wanted to teach it, but she thinks anyone using the above phrases ought to be slapped hard. As you know, The M Club does not condone violence of any kind. (Sara is trying some natural preparations for the night sweats that keep waking her up at night. She should be feeling better soon.)

Session 2 (July 16–August 1) will concentrate on *adding* the following phrases, which are not used enough in our language today:

> "I'm sorry."
>
> "Please forgive me."
>
> "Good job!"
>
> "Thank you."
>
> "God bless you."
>
> "Bless your heart."
>
> "I don't understand, please explain."

Session 2 may not last the entire two weeks. In case students catch on quickly, we will dismiss when everyone has added *all* the phrases to their vocabulary. There is no registration. Just show up at the pond on campus. Bring water; it might be hot.

CHAPTER 9

Fashion

Long before The M Club was officially formed, women like us were making fashion decisions using common sense. It was an M Club type of woman who finally said, "If you think I'm going to put that corset on one more time, you are out of your mind!" Later, M Club types decided it was pretty silly to go swimming with as many clothes on as they usually wore, because too many women were drowning on account of being weighted down by their swimming outfits (layers and layers of heavy fabric, and including hats and shoes).

More recently, women with an M Club attitude were the ones to say, "How on earth did you come up with the idea of a woman's shoe stuck on top of a spike, Mr. Fashion Designer?" And then the M Club women forced the designer's feet into a pair of high heels in an effort to allow him to experience the wonderment of his creation himself. Many of these designers gave up the shoe business after their little chat with The M Club and went into used-car sales.

Current fashion problems are being dealt with by M Club members, because manufacturers and designers appreciate clear, concise opinions in case they don't recognize they are losing money by not fulfilling our needs as M Club women. The M Club's *forty million members* are the ones buying things because we have some money. Besides, some decidedly uncomfortable fashion themes have arisen lately, and The M Club has once again taken on the challenge of getting a few things straightened out around here concerning fashion.

M Club Mandate

The M Club is polling our members on the following mandate before M Club Headquarters issues the new mandate by publishing it in American newspapers. Will the *forty million members* of The M Club (motto: "Because *we* said so!") please cast your vote on whether or not this mandate should be approved? Make your opinion known by M-Mail or e-mail to TheMClub@aol.com whenever you have time. Thank you.

Purpose of Mandate: To inform girls and young women

that there will be no more bare midriffs in public beginning today at 5:00 p.m. EST.

Reasonable Reason for Mandate: The M Club is sick and tired of seeing those flat stomachs with or without rings in the belly buttons. So we contacted all the manufacturers of those half-shirts and got them to admit that they were just trying to save money by selling girls and young women half a shirt! We also contacted the "low on the hips" pants makers, and they finally admitted the same thing!

"We didn't think anybody would notice that we were only using one square foot of fabric instead of enough fabric to cover a whole girl," said one manufacturer, who declined to give his name. "Frankly, when this whole thing started, we had a great big mix-up in the pattern department," he continued, on condition of anonymity. "We had a contract for doll clothes at the same time we got a big contract with a leading young women's clothing store. We accidentally shipped the doll clothes to the popular store and they didn't question us, they just put the teeny, tiny shirts on the mannequins and low and behold, they started selling!"

The M Club thinks that, now that young women know the whole thing was a great big mistake, they will understand the price they are paying for a garment that was made for a doll should not carry the price tag for a whole shirt. We think that if girls knew these facts they might feel taken advantage of as consumers. Also, "low and behold" is supposed to be an expression, *not* a fashion statement!

In our never-ending effort to help other people, The M Club will be demonstrating how we intend to fix this problem, beginning today. We have millions of M Club members who will begin carrying extra blankets, towels, furniture slipcovers, boat cushion material, and bolts of fabric wherever we go. If we see a bare midriff, we will help those girls and young women become aware of their responsibility as future consumers. The M Club is calling our plan "Cover it up or we will cover it for you."

Frankly, The M Club thinks they should all go back to the stores where they bought the half-a-shirt and demand the rest of the shirt or their money back. Another option is to sell the things to a toy store to outfit the dolls they were meant for in the first place. Some of the half-shirts could be used as cloth napkins to set an elegant table! After all, they are the exact same size as a napkin!

Vote now.

M Club Letter

December 3, 2004
Liz Claiborne

Liz,

Please get over there to the manufacturing site where they make the clothes with your name on it and make them stop putting in those crappy shoulder pads. Get over there by 5:00 p.m. EST today.

Liz, M Club members are sick and tired of washing one of your expensive shirts and having the shoulder pads come out all twisted up. Please fix this problem immediately.

We have other things to worry about, and feeling lop-sided because of your damn shoulder pads is not one of them.

So get over there and get those fixed or The M Club will come over there. We will bring all the shoulder pads we have ripped out of the shirts and force you to fix the little holes in our expensive shirts.

Of course, we might just save the trip and go over there to Kmart where Jacqueline Smith has some *better* clothes for *cheaper* prices. Jackie also has plus-size clothing, which M Club members appreciate. The only thing petite about some of us is our opinion of your shirts.

Thanks for taking care of this, Liz.

The M Club

 # M Club Memo

To: All manufacturers of pantyhose
From: The M Club
Att: CEOs

You are hereby notified that it will be unnecessary to continue the manufacture of your "control top" models of pantyhose. In other words, The M Club wants you to *stop making control-top hose.* Stop today. Stop by 4:00 p.m. EST today, please.

We mean any color, any size, with lacy trim or without, any and all hose with any type of control top, including but not limited to firm control, mild control, extra control, caution barrel control, and any others you have over there.

Incidentally, we have never been fond of your sizes. How dare you put us in categories like that. You pretend to be helpful by giving us a chart on the back of the package of pantyhose, and then put us in categories like A, B, C, D, and Q. Don't you have any women working over there to design this product? M Club members *know* our heights as well as our weights. However, following *your* charts, we have wasted a *lot* of money buying hose that you say will fit us but, in fact, will not. The M Club needs you to understand that you may not categorize us with only five capital letters.

We are sick and tired of buying pantyhose according to your measly categories, which will not fit, and then having to figure out another use for them (like "a clever onion bag" or "save soap pieces in there") in our continuing effort to not be wasteful.

We want you to rethink your categories for sizes and send the preliminary ideas to us at TheMClub@aol.com by 3:00 p.m. EST today.

Then we want you to put the brakes on those machines that are making the control-top hose, or whatever you are using over there to put the rubber or elastic or spandex or Lycra or whatever you are using to put the control in the control tops. You have until 4:00 p.m. EST today to put those brakes on or we are coming over there.

Some of us will be red in the face, out of breath, or in actual pain from wearing your dangerous product when we come over there. And if we don't see the new size charts and evidence that you have discontinued the manufacture of the control-top torture devices, we will have a surprise for you.

We will be bringing the thousands of pairs of your hose that we had to rip off in a very last-gasp manner and were never able to face again, and we will be putting them on *you!* Do not doubt that we are able to accomplish this, because we have put many articles of clothing on uncooperative children. We have put diapers, shoes, socks, pants, dresses, coats, mittens, hats, shirts, and undershirts on people who did not want these items put on them. We will have no trouble putting your pantyhose on *you*.

Thanks for taking care of this. See you soon!

M Club Q & A

This question comes from M Club Vice President Alice Springowski:

Q: Dear M Club,
Have any of you women been shopping lately? I went to get some new clothes recently and found a new fashion trend that is both alarming and disturbing. There are a *lot* of "peasant style" clothes being offered, and something needs to be done about it!

Frankly, I already wore peasant shirts back when I was as poor as a peasant when I was younger. However, I have some money now and I don't *want* to wear peasant clothes anymore. Why are they making peasant clothes in women's sizes?

> Alice Springowski
> Los Angeles, California
> M Club VP

A: Dear Alice,
We don't know.

M Club Letter

February 26, 2004
Kaufmann Department Store
Att: Tim Klinger, Manager

Hi Tim,

Thanks so much for making available some good-quality winter coats in February! Yours is one of the few stores where we could even *find* a winter coat to buy in the winter. The M Club hopes your new idea catches on with other stores, and perhaps we will be able to buy seasonal clothing *in season*. We are sick and tired of buying bathing suits in February, because we don't know what size we might be by July!

Also, thanks so much for the great sale you had going yesterday! Who would have thought an upscale clothing store would come up with the idea of a "buy one get one free" sale for coats? Usually this type of sale is reserved for toothpaste or paper towels or something we really can use. What a clever market-ing effort it is for you to sell *$300 all-wool coats* using this "buy one get one free" gimmick. Great idea, Tim.

However, The M Club wants you to think this through a little more, please. Tim, who would buy *two* floor-length, fully lined, snappy wool coats at the same time? Are you privy to some weather forecasting that we need to know about? If not, please explain how you are able to give away one of your great coats.

Of course, we realize that by offering one for free, you are simply reducing the price by half. But the coats were also on sale at a reduced price (around $100 each), so we need to know how you can sell two coats for $50 each. You are also offering some of those coupons that come in the mail that give us another 15 percent off.

To recap: On February 25, 2003, I was able to purchase two gorgeous high-quality wool coats valued at $600 yesterday for $85. If I paid $85 for one, you gave me the other one free today.

Tim, a free coat is a free coat. If it is free today, it should have been free yesterday or the day before or on December 24. And if that is the case, a *lot* of people could have gotten a nice coat for Christmas. But they didn't. They had to wear the same old beige coat with the pocket lining stained with blue ink. They had already had to replace two buttons, which didn't match exactly. In addition, beige has never been "their color."

The M Club is *comin' over there* tomorrow, Tim. Please have *all* those coats put into those fancy zippered bags by 2:00 p.m. EST. We will pick up those free coats and *give* them to people who need one. Most of these people will say, "My beige coat is fine, really. I can get another year out of it, I'm sure." But we are going to make them take a new coat because most people don't argue with us when we give them *The M Club Glare.*

We will be sure and tell them the new coats are from you, Tim. And we are positive you will not have to worry about anyone exchanging one of those free coats, because when most people receive a gift, they know it is impolite to exchange it.

See you around 1:30 p.m. EST! Debi says to please have some hot, *fresh* coffee for The M Club when we get there. Maybe you could use one of those $400 coffeemakers you have up there on the second floor. Use what you want, though, just make sure it is ready when we get there. We like Colombian because it is strong, like us.

See you then, and thanks!

The M Club

M Club Letter

February 29, 2004
No Excuses Jeans
Att: Cindy Hooker, CEO

Hi Cindy,

The M Club loves your product name for your blue jeans and shirts! We have said "No Excuses!" for years and years whenever we are forced to stand there and listen to the reasons people have for not doing the right thing.

Anyway, we want you to change the *sizes only* on a bunch of your blue jeans and any other pants you have over there. We want a good selection of men's, women's, boy's, and girl's jeans marked with different sizes.

To be more clear: Lay out about ten pairs of your regular "No Excuses" men's size 34 x 32 jeans on a table. Now, rip off the tag that says "34 x 32." Then, please put a new tag on these pants: "size 38 x 30."

Have you got it? Put tags with bigger sizes on the smaller pants. If you have questions, e-mail us at TheMClub@aol.com and we will walk you through the procedure.

Okay, now do the same thing for all the sizes.

We can't think of a better way to get our message across that a *lot* of people are *too big for their britches.* We have tried explaining the concept to them when they act too big for their britches, when they are unkind, downright mean, or generally unconcerned about another person's feelings. But lectures don't work as well as demonstrations!

The M Club will be sending a *lot* of new customers to you. Please have your salespeople standing by to say, "Looks like you are *too big for your britches!*" when they come out of the dressing room and seem confused about their pants not fitting. They will get the idea.

The **M** Club

CHAPTER 10

Current M Club Projects

> "We have the experience and tenacity to take care of a few things we see wrong around here. So we do."

The M Club is working on some big projects to take care of a few things we see wrong around here. Because of our age, imagination, and experience, we are good at helping out. M Club chapters from all over are letting us know what projects they are working on. We hope more new M Club chapters are being formed right this minute and that they will also send us their opinions, rants, celebrity interviews, consumer ideas, inventions, "Because She's

My Friend" stories, and recipes to TheMClub@aol.com. Send us your press releases on new classes offered by The M Club in your area. After all, we're all in this together.

We will keep you informed of our progress on big issues and little issues through our weekly syndicated newspaper column distributed by Universal Press Syndicate beginning in the fall of 2004. Be sure and let us know what you're doing and if you need any help. The M Club will *come over there.* We have cars.

Meanwhile, here are a few projects in the works:

M CLUB PROJECT FROM KANSAS CiTY, MiSSOURi, CHAPTER

December 1, 2004

Dear Marlo,

So good to see you again as Rachael's mother on *Friends.* Your acting abilities are as sharp as ever and you look great.

Mar, The M Club needs to know how many of your old *Kids Are People Too* books are still being sold. Also, please tell us how many you think are still circulating in libraries. How many copies do you have and how many did you give as gifts?

The M Club thinks too many people got the wrong message from your book. The M Club believes *Kids Are People*

When We Say They Are People Too. If you had called your book by this title, we might have a few less problems around here right now. Could there have been a mix-up at the printers?

It is not your fault that children got the wrong idea about this. As far as we know, kids try to skip around while they are reading and might have missed some important points. Did you mean to give children the impression that they were the *same* as adults? Please explain.

The M Club thinks some of those kids who read your old book might have gotten that impression, and we are sure you agree with us when we say, "Boy, are they wrong!"

Since you are still acting, we are wondering if you are still in the publishing game as well. We feel it is up to you to create, publish, and distribute an updated version of that old book. Maybe you could put fewer words in this one. Please make sure there is no way anyone reading your new book comes away with the impression that kids have the same rights as adults; that kids are entitled to speak to adults like they are grown up already; or that kids are people too until we let them know they are only people when they begin to *act* like the rest of us. Of course, sometimes this takes years and years. And years.

Feel free to use our suggested title, *Kids Are People When We Tell Them They Are People Too,* or make up a title on your own. We don't care what you call your new book, but we want to see some preliminary ideas by 9:00 p.m.

EST on Tuesday, March 18, 2005. E-mail them to M Club Headquarters at TheMClub@aol.com.

Thanks for taking care of this, honey. Looking forward to your new ideas by Tuesday!

The M Club
Kansas City Chapter

P.S. Hello to Phil!

M CLUB PROJECT FROM KEY WEST, FLORIDA, CHAPTER

Dear M Club Headquarters:

We are working on an article to dispute those little books that were titled *Don't Sweat the Small Stuff.* Those little books swayed public opinion for a while and gave us all a break from too much stress. They were useful and appreciated at the time. However, our M Club members have noticed some important things were getting lumped in with "the small stuff," which we don't think should be in that category.

We think that sometimes "the small stuff" can make a big difference in how people treat each other.

Our M Club chapter is having trouble with the title because none of us thinks "sweat" is a very delicate word. We are in favor of the word "perspire."

We will keep working on the article and worry about the title later.

Sincerely,
Jan Jeavons
M Club VIP, Key West

M CLUB PROJECT FROM NEW HAMPSHIRE CHAPTER

Hi, Prez,

Here is our report for the project we are working on. As soon as we hear from the governor we will let you know if we will have to *go over there.*

Gov. Craig Benson
Office of the Governor
25 Capitol Street
Concord, NH 03301 USA

Hi, Craig,

Please tell us how much money you have collected for your plan to glue the rocks that fell down last May back onto the mountain. We are aware that many people in our great state are very upset about the Old Man in the Mountain succumbing to natural erosion, but The M Club thinks there might be something better to do with the money you are collecting to put the face back on the rocks.

The newspapers said you "quickly declared that the face should be 'revitalized.'" Have you had time to think this over? After all, M Club members have found out that even when we get our faces "revitalized," it is only a matter of time before a face will fall again!

The paper also said you were "planning to meet with state officials to determine how it should be done and planned to form a fund to take donations." We hope you meet with one of your state officials named Lance dePlante. He is the director of the your Office of Homeless and Housing Services. His office might even be right near your office.

It is up to you to find out where Lance's office is located. Please go over to Lance's office by 1:00 p.m. EST today (right after lunch). We made an appointment for you. Lance has a lot of statistics in his office. Here is one: "Last year, more than 6,800 individuals were served in 41 state-funded homeless shelters—up 8.5 percent over the previous year. *But over 13,500 were turned away because the shelters were full.*"

Craig, maybe if you talked to Lance about some *real* old men and women who were turned away from homeless shelters, you wouldn't feel so upset about the figurative Old Man of the Mountain, which was, after all, just some rocks. The outcropping that fell down didn't even look that much like an old man, in our opinion. But there are some real men and women and children who could probably use the money you are collecting to put the rocks back. Could you ask Lance about it, please?

Looking forward to hearing from you by 2:00 p.m. EST.

The M Club
New Hampshire Chapter

M CLUB PROJECT FROM WASHINGTON, D.C., CHAPTER

Because this chapter of The M Club is located so close to lawmakers, it has chosen a project that could save time in case they have to *go over there* to have a little chat in person. It began as a discussion over margaritas and other M Club drinks, including but not limited to: Manhattans, Martinis, Meyers, Molson, Michelob, Mai Tais, Moet, Modelo, Mondavi, Mojitos. The M Club D.C. motto is: "A drink is a drink. Just make it wet."

The D.C. chapter of The M Club has been wondering if it isn't time to reevaluate the list of grounds for divorce in the American justice system. After all, it has been a new millennium for a couple of years already and a *lot* of things are still the same.

So these women are presenting a case to the Supreme Court. M Club members always go right to the top. At the very least, they want the highest court in the land to consider expanding the situations under the heading "irreconcilable differences."

From their report:

> The M Club has a lot of members who need to know if some of the following situations could please be considered as grounds for divorce under the heading "irreconcilable differences":

- My husband likes to invite friends over for get-togethers frequently. He usually tells me about a party a day before he has already invited people. When I get that deer-in-the-headlights look on my face, he says, "Not to worry! I will *help* you get ready!" While I rush around getting food, drink, and the house ready, he *helps* by going out and trimming the bushes. He says this must be done before the party (even though the guests will arrive after dark and won't even *see* the landscaping), and I say someone needs to clean the bathroom. Is this an irreconcilable difference and is it grounds for divorce?

- My husband is a great handyman! He has a big list of small projects around the house. Because he is so handy, I asked him to put up a new shelf in the kitchen for me. I asked him every day for a week. He said it was not on "his list." He knows I am sick and tired of lists. Is this grounds for divorce?

- My husband had a mid-life crisis and bought a BMW at the same time our two sons were moving away to college. The payments are a real stretch, especially because education is so expensive. Am I allowed to use a sports car as grounds for divorce? If so, may I please have a note to send to BMW telling them I don't have to make the payment while the car is "named as a defendant in a divorce action"?

• For twenty-two years I have sat across from a man who cannot eat a spoonful of soup without blowing on it. This includes chowders, stews, and regular soups. He doesn't just blow on each spoonful once; he blows on each spoonful three times before he puts it in his mouth. Would you call this an irreconcilable difference?

• Please tell me if a man has a right to claim he is from another planet in an effort to keep our marriage together. I have slept in the same bed with this guy for thirty years, and I have never witnessed anything extraterrestrial about him at all. Not once. Yet, he bought a lot of books that he says explain the way he is, and he offers them as proof that he can't help being the way he is. I told him I didn't care what planet he thought he was from; we are both living on Earth right now so he had better stop blaming his shortcomings on being from Pluto (maybe it was Jupiter or Mercury, I can't remember). If he is so convinced he is from another planet, is this an irreconcilable difference? After all, I thought I married an American.

• Please consider adding socks to your list of irreconcilable differences.

The M Club will keep members informed of the Supreme Court's decision on adding allowable issues as possible irreconcilable differences. Meanwhile, use this handy M Club Scales of Justice to weigh your own predicament.

He still makes me laugh ~ Party preparations
He has to work a *lot* ~ Not so handy
He smells nice sometimes ~ BMW
He can cook if he wants to ~ Soup eating
He knows the names of his children ~ Extraterrestrial excuse
We are beginning to look alike ~ Socks

M CLUB PROJECT FROM DAYTON, OHIO, CHAPTER

Hello, Fellow M Club Members!

We are a small group of women who are definitely *in* The M Club. In fact, we used to be a book club, but we got sick and tired of reading books and talking about them and not *doing anything with all of our experience and tenacity.* So we joined the Club and have decided our first order of business is to remind other readers of some of our great M Club writers.

We chose this project because it has come to our attention that junior members of The M Club are unaware of some of our great M Club writers. Many M Club members were in conversation with younger members recently, when they mentioned Erma. The younger members *all* said, "Erma who?"

When the shock wore off, senior M Club members educated these younger women about Erma. We think there might be a *lot* of younger women who need to know about Erma.

We want all M Club members who know about Erma to tell other M Club members a couple of Erma stories. You can say something like: "When my kids were little and I was overwhelmed and wanted to cry, I picked up any one of Erma's books and I laughed. I laughed out loud. Sometimes I laughed so hard I cried. I felt a lot better about everything because of Erma."

Or you may say, "Erma is the one who told us all not to sweat the small stuff. Much later, those little books came out about not sweating the small stuff, but Erma had the idea first."

You could even say, "It was Erma's idea to fashion a basketball hoop over her clothes hampers in an effort to get her kids to put dirty clothes where they belong (it didn't work). You might have seen that gag on many television sitcoms, but it was Erma's idea. She wrote about that a long time ago."

Or say, "Without Erma, I don't know if I could have survived. She had the same problems that I had, and when she told a story about what she was going through she made it so funny that I saw the humor in the situation. She taught me how to look for the humor in a *lot* of situations, and I will forever be in her debt."

We are not telling the women the titles of Erma's books. We think those girls should go find her books on their own. They will see how many, many books Erma wrote. They will find books from every stage of family life and beyond. Let them choose where to start. We aren't telling younger M Club members they have to read Erma's books in any type of order. Order did not matter to Erma and it does not matter to us. Even Erma's oldest books still ring true, because she wrote in a universal language. She wrote from her heart. Everything she wrote still applies.

One last thing, Club members. We are not letting on that Erma is gone. She is not gone. She lives in our hearts and our minds. She is with all of us still. We will never forget how much we owe Erma for helping us through all those tough times. A lot of women say, "I will laugh about this someday." But Erma made us laugh *today*. She didn't think we should have to wait.

So don't wait to tell somebody about Erma. Do it today. Do it by 5:00 p.m. EST, please. It would be great, when you tell somebody about Erma, if you could lend them a book or two from your collections.

Our next project will be the same kind of thing, only next time we will highlight Jean Kerr!

M CLUB PROJECT FROM M CLUB HEADQUARTERS

M Club members here at headquarters are in the process of contacting famous women who have proven their membership in The M Club. Even if Oprah doesn't call, perhaps Ellen, Carrie, Goldie, Diane, Laura, Sissy, Susan, Bette, etc., will agree to an interview. Until then, we know a *lot* of celebrities. These are remarkable women who may not be famous but have the grace, style, attitude, and same sense of humor enjoyed by most M Club members.

M Club Celebrity Interview

Today's celebrity is Mary L. Stewart.
Mary is a celebrity because she is eighty-five years old and goes to her tai chi class every Tuesday night. She is smart and funny and she could kick your butt, so we think she is a celebrity.

M CLUB PRESIDENT: Welcome, Mary, and thank you for speaking with us today!

Mary: Thank you. I always make time to share thoughts with fellow M Club members, when I am asked, of course. I hardly ever give my opinion if I am not asked for it, though.

M CLUB PRESIDENT: Are you saying that you have learned in your eighty-five years that most people simply want to be listened to instead of bombarded with opinions and unsolicited advice?

MARY: Yes. I have wasted a lot of things, but I rarely waste my breath. I have wasted money, time, paper, tears, and a *lot* of other things, but I do not waste breath because I need it for my tai chi exercises.

M CLUB PRESIDENT: Speaking of paper, weren't you the first woman sportswriter for the *Cleveland News*? The one who covered the Cleveland Indians in 1948 when they won the pennant and went to the World Series?

MARY: Yes. I sort of got the job because all the male sportswriters were at war. I enjoyed it, though, and I am still an avid Indians fan to this day. My collection of memorabilia from those days is valuable to me. I don't care how much *money* it is worth, but it is valuable because I take it around to show to schoolchildren as an interesting history lesson.

M CLUB PRESIDENT: What else did you write for the paper?

MARY: I did a lot of things. I reported on crimes, government meetings, and social events. Women always wore their hats and gloves downtown then. When the editors needed a model for a refrigerator ad, they took my picture standing next to appliances. I was glad to do it because it was standing still instead of running around gathering news! Then I married a doctor, had four children, and worked at my father's printing and publishing company. I still write and edit books for our local historical society and write feature articles for the local newspaper.

M CLUB PRESIDENT: You certainly keep busy, Mary!

MARY: Well, of course. There is a *lot* to do, a lot to learn, a *lot* of people to help, and none of us gets a *lot* of time. Surely everyone knows this?

M CLUB PRESIDENT: Now we do. Thank you for speaking with us today, Mary.

MARY: Anytime. Would you like to go to my tai chi class with me tonight? It is Tuesday.

M CLUB PRESIDENT: I would love to. We could call it *Tuesdays with Mary.*

MARY: Wait until you see me swing my broad sword. See you at seven tonight?

M CLUB PRESIDENT: I wouldn't miss it for the world. See you then.

M CLUB PROJECT FROM
DALLAS, TEXAS, CHAPTER

Dallas, TX—New and exciting classes will be offered at Southern Methodist University next semester. The M Club Dallas Chapter is sponsoring the classes, which are free.

CAPACITY FOR LEARNING

This class is for all people who believe they do not have the capacity to learn anything new just because they are out of school. Members of The M Club will teach students what the real capacity for learning is, where it comes from, and what to do with all that capacity.

Students will learn that there is still plenty of room in the old brain for much new knowledge. People who think they have filled up all the nooks and crannies of their craniums will learn that their brains are not really out of space; it is a filing system and storage problem.

Students will learn that it is easy to delete old, bitter memories and free up space. Up to eight gazillion hepabites can be freed up by deleting bad childhood memories alone. This is a lot of space to put new information in.

Students will learn once and for all that, like a lot of things, size doesn't really matter. God gave us all pretty much the same size brains. Some of us are not using enough hepabites hiding in those cranny nooks.

There is no registration. Interested participants should walk around the gorgeous campus and be on the lookout for people who look like they are thinking. Don't worry. You will find each other. As soon as prospective students decide to take this class, start thinking about what you might want to bring. Bring it. Think of it as your first homework assignment. See you at SMU.

M CLUB PROJECT FROM
FLAGSTAFF, ARIZONA, CHAPTER

Grand Canyon National Park—We hope you can join us at rim-side for two exciting new classes offered this winter. M Club classes are free because we feel education has gotten way too expensive. There is no registration because we are sick and tired of keeping track of names on lists. We have kept track of our children, our husbands, our dog's medications, and shoes for other people. We are also sick and tired of lists.

EASIER SAID THAN DONE

This class will explore the truth to the saying "Easier said than done." Of course, it is true. Students will learn that saying anything is very, very easy. Students will then learn that getting something done is a *lot* tougher, especially because it requires action of some kind.

The class is being held on the rim so we can use the beautiful Grand Canyon as a visual aide. M Club teachers will point to the canyon and make analogies like: God might have said, "I think I will create the most special place in America where everyone from all over the world can come and see grandeur at its finest. I will make rivers and canyons and snow-capped peaks and sprinkle wild columbine plants around by the millions and put lots of trees there and make the air very special too."

God might have said it first, but then he did it. Hence the saying, "Easier said than done."

Students will also learn that saying something and doing it are two different things. We will prove that there is little reward in saying something, anything, unless students plan on following through and getting it done.

Students who continually say they will do something and then don't follow through and get it done will be held after class.

Hope to see you at the canyon rim, by the pond, on December 24. Dress warmly. The air will be cold, but it will sure remind participants they are alive.

POINT OF VIEW

A continuation of "Easier Said Than Done." This class will demonstrate many points of view. The location is the same—meet at the rim of the Grand Canyon by the pond. Please wear layered clothing. Students will be moving around a lot to see different issues from different points of view. The view here is great. It is easy to see different points of view from here.

Hot cocoa and a campfire will be enjoyed by all. John Denver fans may bring the marshmallows.

M CLUB PROJECT FROM
SEATTLE, WASHiNGTON, CHAPTER

The M Club in Seattle will begin collecting all the bullets we have been biting over the years. We will collect them starting today at 2:00 p.m. EST. Please bring your bitten bullets to the town square or the biggest statue in the city where you live to turn in those bullets.

We want the bullets you bit when you paid those extra taxes, as well as the bullets you bit while conceding that argument with the in-laws even though it turns out you were right. We want the bitten bullets from the doctor's office when you decided to go with the treatment suggested and had to bite the bullet and just do it. Also, please send the bullets you bit while trying to advise a teenager that you really did know best from personal experience, and then had to bite a great big bullet and let him/her find out for himself.

We are collecting *any kind* of bullets you bit.

The M Club knows there are millions of bitten bullets out there, from all the times we have been forced to "bite the bullet."

Guess what! We are planning on melting down all those dented bullets with all the bite marks on them and doing something *useful* with all that metal. Let's face it: Unless you are planning on crowning your own teeth with that metal, you will have no use for the bullets you have bitten for years and years. And years.

So gather up all those bullets and take them to The M Club collection center today! As soon as we have collected a good supply, we will announce plans for what we intend to do with the melted metal.

We have suggestions from M Club members already, including but not limited to:

- Free braces for children
- Hum-V molds that will encase any model of car to better protect inexperienced drivers from senior citizen drivers
- A donation to the Department of Defense

If you have a suggestion on what we can do with all the bullets we have bitten over the years, send your suggestion to TheMClub@aol.com. Thanks.

M CLUB PROJECT FROM BOSTON, MASSACHUSETTS, CHAPTER

IMU—The M Club in Boston will teach a refresher course at our new university, IMU (I Am You). In case you didn't know or used to know but somehow forgot, The M Club does not charge for classes because (a) education has gotten way too expensive, (b) we are sick and tired of keeping track of names on lists (we have kept track of our children, our husbands, pinking sheers that are not even pink, and shoes for other people); and (c) we know how to teach.

THE DROP AND RUN will be taught on August 2, 2005, from 11:00 a.m. EST to 4:00 p.m. EST. In case you can't make it there by 11:00 a.m. EST, you are invited to the other class, "Drop Everything and Get There as Soon as I Can" at noon (EST).

Most M Club members already know how to drop everything and *run* at a moment's notice. We have all had a *lot* of experience in this technique. This class is not to be confused with the program taught by the fire department called "Stop, Drop, and Roll." You cannot get someplace at record speed if you waste time rolling around.

We will discuss the many situations in which we have been forced to *drop and run*, including but not limited to:

- Blood-curdling screams from our own children

- Blood-curdling screams from someone else's children

- A phone call from a friend who, even though she said you need not come over, you could tell by her voice that you need to go over there

- A phone call from a friend who is sobbing hysterically and asking you to come (Note: Find out who is calling. Hysterical sobbing sounds alike in many M Club members. Do not assume. Say, "Yes. I am coming! Who is this?" Then proceed with the *drop and run*.)

After a short break, with lunch provided by The M Club, we will go over the specific situations you may or may not be busy attending to when you *drop everything and run.* Students will learn that there is nothing so important that it can't wait. If there is a friend in need, *just go.*

Students will learn that a lack of transportation is not a hindrance to the *drop and run.* M Club members have successfully gotten places when we didn't have a car *or* a bike. Meet by the pond at IMU. Please wear comfortable clothing as we will be practicing the one-hundred-yard dash for the *run* procedure. Also, please bring something to *drop.* In case it is 90 degrees or above, Debi says we will modify the class and practice the "drop everything and *walk* as fast as we can." Meet by the pond.

Hope you can join us.